THE DOT WROTE THE NAME SO WE CAN READ IT

THE NAME

KHAL SALEM (ALKARKARI)

Published by Hemingway Publishers

Cover design by Hemingway Publishers

ISBN: Printed in the United States

In the name of Allah, the Most Merciful, the Most Compassionate.

May Allah bless, send gratitude upon, and establish our connection with the Prophet Muhammad and his family.

Dedication

Dedication to Sheikh Muhammad Faouzi Al-Karkari

Acknowledgments

- I believe that simply expressing gratitude is not enough to truly honour my spiritual mentor and Godfather, Sheikh Muhammad Faouzi Al-Karkari.
- I would also like to thank my late mentor from Egypt, Sheikh Saad Rashad.
- To my colleague and professional beta reader, Jennifer Smith, for the valuable feedback and support input.
- To my godchildren, Emma and Abdellah Al-Karkari, thank you for your thoughtful brainstorming and review ideas.
- I would like to thank the mother of my children, Beki, and my children, Meryam, Zak, and Essie, for their support with my first book and as I move forward with my current one.

Table of Content

Introduction

The path to God is significantly simplified and inherent in the names He has revealed to us. This escalating revelation of names culminated in the final name accompanying the last message, which is Allah (الله).

The journey from ignorance to gnosis lies in the name of *Allah* (الله), leading to the knowledge of the Creator. This contrasts with the structured religious journey of rituals and the shift from physical to metaphysical understanding, ultimately leading to divine awareness.

This book employs a distinct style that blends characteristics of Arabic lettering to illuminate the spiritual navigation journey along a path within the name of Allah in Arabic script (الله). Even Arabic speakers may find this knowledge unfamiliar.

> - I highly encourage readers to familiarize themselves with name tracing and the visual characteristics of Arabic letters. This involves observing, tracing, pronouncing, and then closing your eyes to recall the traced image. Readers must remember that Arabic is written from right to left.

Seven-Step Approach to Becoming Acquainted with the Majestic Name

Step 1 – First Letter (Aleph):

1. Trace your index finger from top to bottom, then return from bottom to top. Interestingly, pronunciation may differ based on tracing direction, resembling the difference between the English letters 'a' and 'e'.

2. Say "Aleph" aloud to hear it.

3. Shut your eyes.

4. Visualize and mentally trace the letter bidirectionally while saying "Aleph."

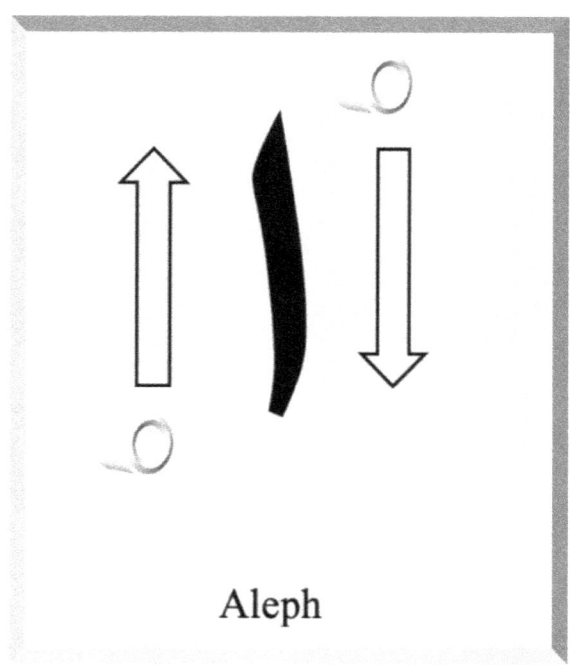

Aleph

Step 2 – Second Letter (Lam):

1. Trace the letter from top to bottom with your index finger.

2. Say "Lam" aloud to hear it.

3. Shut your eyes.

4. Visualize and mentally trace the image while saying "Lam."

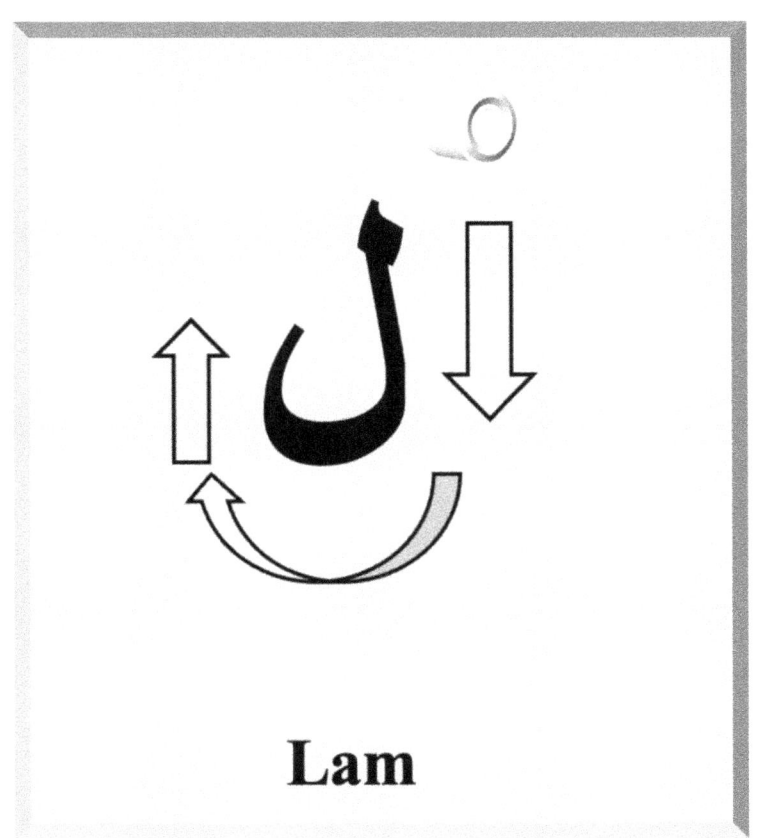

Lam

Step 3 – Duplicated Third Letter (Lam):

Repeat the above steps

Lam

Step 4 – Fourth Letter (Ha):

1. Trace the letter with your index finger all around, starting from any point.

2. Say "Ha" aloud so that you can hear it.

3. Shut your eyes.

4. Visualize and mentally trace the letter circumferentially while saying "Ha."

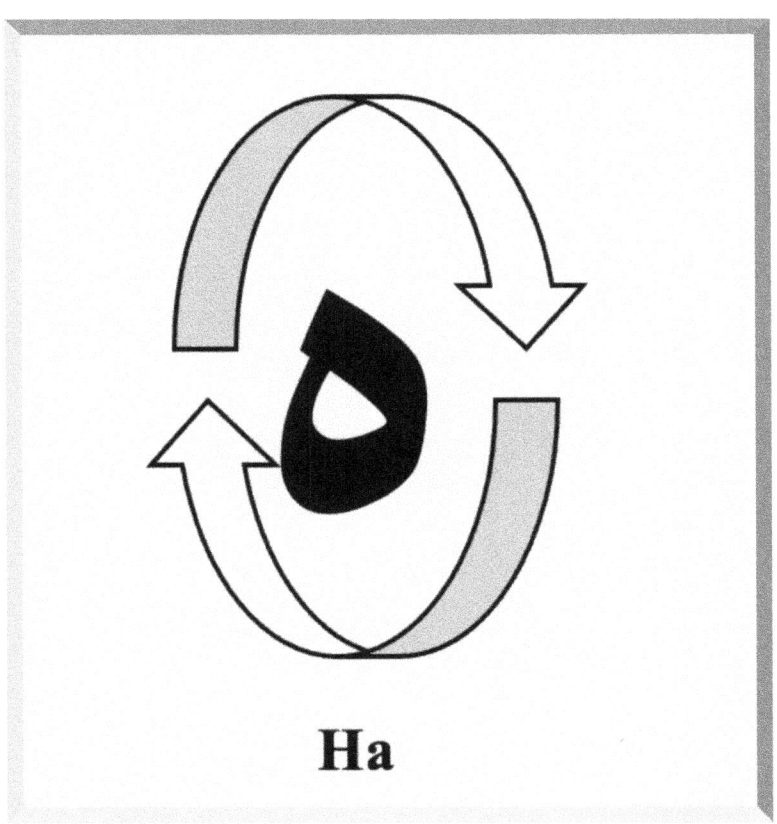

Ha

Step 5 – Entire Name:

1. Trace the entire name.

2. Say: Allah

3. Shut your eyes.

4. Visualize and repeat the name from the dot to the circle, moving from right to left.

Allah

Step 6 – The Navigation Path:

Visualize the navigation path from left to right, from the center of the Ha to the midpoint of the Aleph.

The Name as a Navigation Path (Sulook)

Step 7 – Memorization:

Repeat these steps until you can mentally trace and recall the four letters every time you reopen the book and at the beginning of every chapter.

> # The Dot Wrote the Name So We Can Read It

Chapter 1
The Name

If there's one consensus among humanity, it is that naming is crucial for identifying entities.

Expectant parents relish finding a distinctive name for their future child.

In non-scientific literature, referring to things without naming them signifies a lack of eloquence. In contrast, in scientific literature, using pronouns such as he, she, or it when exclusively referring to a name reflects a humble admission of ignorance or suggests a need for further research.

Conversely, poetry presents a different approach— referencing without revealing the name or using metaphors instead. That is why the language of scientific literature sometimes clashes with, and at times undermines, intriguing non-scientific or poetic works.

Subsequently, the variability in people's methods of perceiving names—directly, through pronouns, or via poetic hints—serves as a broad reflection of naming.

Spiritually speaking, truth seekers (spiritual navigators) tend to be lumpers rather than dispersers. They seek the collective SECRET of their Creator's name—which the Creator gave to Himself—and explore its significance.

People assigned the name God to refer to Him. In Sufi literature, the pronoun 'He' (هو) serves the same purpose and is also considered a name of the Divine Essence. Understanding God's name should suffice to answer every question.

Truth seekers strive to deeply comprehend what the name implies and delve into its non-tangible driving momentum. Sufism refers to this as the SECRET or the HIDDEN SECRET.

This secret, and what is even more hidden, is mentioned in the Qur'an:

"He certainly knows the secret and what is even more hidden."

(Surah Ṭā-Hā, 20:7)

"Say, it has been revealed by the One who knows the secret of the heavens and the earth. Surely, He is All-Forgiving, Most Merciful."

(Surah Al-Furqān, 25:6)

Divine Ink, the Sea, and the Pen

How does the creation process flow through the invincibility **(Jabarūt)** aspect of divine name revelation?

This requires further exploration of certain verses in the Qur'an.

The analogy of the sea and divine words—and the supply of ink—is presented in:

"Say, if the ocean were ink for 'writing' the Words of my Lord, it would certainly run out before the Words of my Lord were finished, even if We refilled it with its equal."

(Surah Al-Kahf, 18:109)

Surah Luqmān explores the concept of pen replication using the analogy of trees:

"If all the trees on earth were pens and the ocean were filled with seven other oceans, the Words of Allah would not be exhausted. Surely Allah is Almighty, All-Wise."

(Surah Luqmān, 31:27)

The Primary Pen is referenced in various verses:

"Nun. By the pen and what they inscribe!"

(Surah Al-Qalam, 68:1)

This verse hints that the last letter of the Divine word that ignited the Pen to write is Nun (ن).

The first letter of the Divine command is found in:

"Indeed, Our Quote, if will something 'to exist', We say: 'Be,' and it is."

(Surah An-Naḥl, 16:40)

The Arabic word **"Be"** is pronounced **"Kun"** (كن). Therefore, the first letter of the all-encompassing Divine word is **Kāf** (ك).

Highlights of the Summary

- The dot of ink shapes the scripted letters.
- Letters are mere illusions created by the movement of this dot.
- The ink's dot represents a secret.
- The abundance of ink dots is beautifully illustrated in the Qur'an, where it is described as a sea or ocean.

- Divine words are the secret of the secret manifested through the ink (مداد).
- Writing the divine words requires a pen analogy for the mind to understand.
- Primary pen and replicated pens possess different functions.
- The primary pen is depicted as a tree, while the replicated pens are shown as the branches of this tree in the Quran.
- The word Be or Kun (كن) is the all-inclusive Divine word that carries the momentum of the secret of the secret.

The Dot Wrote the Name so We Can Read It

Chapter 2
The Letters

The Dot. The Sea. The Pen

The letters are symbols created by the original, mysterious ink dot, demonstrating its unlimited capabilities.

Here is a theme to visualize this intricate topic:

- Visualize an ocean of divine words.

- A pen is ready to write, dipped into the ocean, and has grabbed a drop of ink.

- The pen releases the original drop of ink to create a dot.

- This dot, originating from the ocean, moves by default.

- The dot uncovers the exciting revelation that Allah's characteristics, names, and attributes are displayed exponentially—multiplying by manifesting themselves in countless, indefinite forms.

The initial writing was a straight line.

In our physical realm, this straight line is represented by the number 1 and the letter Aleph.

We can confidently state that the creation process is uniquely represented by the number one (1), and all letters are variations of the Aleph.

Hence, the science of numerology originated where Aleph = 1, Ba = 2, Jeem = 3, etc.

This table illustrates the concept of multiplication and the basics of numerology.

The numerology system in Arabic is decimal-based, and the base of the numerical tree ranges from 1 to 9. What is beyond 9 necessitates the presence of nonexistence.

The Arabs invented the number zero from a metaphysical understanding of the need for nothingness—to illustrate the illusion of multiplication.

The concept of multiplicity is derived from adding zero or more. It supports the Muslim approach to numerology and emphasizes that unity and singularity are essential for validating divine wisdom.

This notion is articulated through monotheistic and polytheistic numerological references, reflecting the distinction between worshiping the one true God and associating partners with Him.

Arabic Letters & Numerological Values

Numeric Value	Binary Form	Transliteration	Letter
1	1	Aleph	ا
2	11	Ba`	ب
3	111	Jeem	ج
4	1111	Dal	د
5	11111	Ha	ه
6	111111	Wao	و
7	1111111	Zain	ز
8	11111111	Hha`	ح
9	111111111	Dta`	ط
10	1111111111	Ya`	ي
20	1111111111 X 2	Kaf	ك
30	1111111111 X 3	Lam	ل
40	1111111111 X 4	Meem	م
50	1111111111 X 5	Nun	ن
60	1111111111 X 6	Seen	س
70	1111111111 X 7	A`in	ع
80	1111111111 X 8	Fa`	ف

90	1111111111 X 9	Suad	ص
100	1111111111 X 10	Qaaf	ق
200	1111111111 X 20	Ra`	ر
300	1111111111 X 30	Sheen	ش
400	1111111111 X 40	Ta`	ت
500	1111111111 X 50	Tha`	ث
600	1111111111 X 60	Kha`	خ
700	1111111111 X 70	Zthal	ذ
800	1111111111 X 80	Dhad	ض
900	1111111111 X 90	Dtha`	ظ
1000	1111111111 X 100	Ghayn	غ

Using numerology to calculate the numerological reference to the name Allah is calculated this way:

Aleph (ا) + Lam (ل) + Lam (ل) + Ha (ه)

$= 1 + 30 + 30 + 5$

$= 66$

This 66 can be simplified to:

$6 + 6 = 12 \rightarrow 1 + 2 = 3$

- The dot's representation of multiple 'digit ones' predates the representation of letters.
- Numbers embody the essence and secret of creativity, expressed in letters and creation.
- The smaller the number, the more magnificent the creation displayed. For example, based on and originating from 7, the Seven Heavens exist due to multiplication in their creations. Thus, the small number creates a larger spatial expanse.
- Values less than 10 align more closely with reality.
- The truth lies between 1 and 9, as they don't rely on zero to define reality by multiplying illusory forms.

Spiritual Context:

The spiritual navigator defines monotheism as the journey back from the many to the original One—a process referred to as Tawheed.

Letters, therefore, are considered the dot's attire, conveying its indefinite characters.

Thus, the trace of the name Allah (الله) is the dot's allure, conveying the essential characteristics of Allah through motion.

The dot also becomes the pen's disclosing means. Functioning as both ink and pen, it showcases the mysterious characteristics of the primordial dot.

On the Pen and Creation:

In a narrated hadeeth, the first thing Allah created was the PEN.

"The first entity Allah created was the Pen; He commanded it, 'Write,' and all beings came into existence."

— *Hadith, Al-Tirmidhi*

Further, in sources such as the tradition books Al-Tabari and Al-Hakim, Ibn Abbas added:

"Then water steam was elevated to create the skies, and a letter shaped like 'Nun' (ن) created the earth; Nun is an Arabic letter that looks like a deep bowl with a dot in the periphery.

The impact of this motion is the creation and indefinite duplication of countless replicas of the Dot's attire. This replication is referred to in Sufism as *Tajalli* (manifestation).

This term is used in:

"And when his Lord manifested Himself to the mountain, He made it crumble to dust, and Moses fell unconscious."

— Surah Al-A'raf, *7:143*

Therefore, the origin and reality are one, and replication is the illusion that created the cosmos, its forms, and shapes. This makes the Dot the only soul in the universal structures and bodies.

Everything embodies the Dot, reflecting one of its characteristics by showcasing the dot's beauty or, at times, representing degrees of exact opposites.

Allah possesses sentimental attributes that He uniquely understands. Since He permitted others to exist as reflections of His name's manifestations, the illusory reality of others necessitates another illusion for learning through contrast.

The illusions are described in the Quran as the qualities of Satan. In Surah Fatir, Allah says:

10

"O humanity! Indeed, Allah's promise is true. So do not let the life of this world deceive you (delude you), nor let the Chief Deceiver (The Illusionist) deceive you about Allah."

— Qur'an, *35:5*

In addition, Satan represents evil and is likened to a wandering illusionist whose possessions comprise illusory bags or luggage.

In Surah Al-Hadid:

"The life of this world is nothing but the illusion of enjoyment."

(— Qur'an, *57:20*).

Allah is good, but the illusory 'others' (Aghyar; أغيار) are educated about lordship through reverse embodiments of the Dot manifesting evil in the physical realm, which accommodates all opposites; in contrast, the spiritual world allows only beauty and goodness to exist outside.

This may answer some of the Epicurean Paradox mentioned previously.

As an opposing embodiment of goodness, Satan was allowed to remain in the higher illuminated world only when he did not act on his evil qualities; however, when he employed his wicked skills to allure Adam, he had to descend to the physical realm to learn about himself and experience what pride, arrogance, innocence, and hate mean.

This descent made him learn more about himself. *"Then get down from Paradise! It is not for you to be arrogant here. So get out! You are truly one of the disgraced."*

— Surah Al-A'raf, *7:13*

Even though Satan knew he was cursed, he accepted the inevitable and even asked for more. Learning about himself, Satan entered an intoxicated state; he requested to extend his curse until the day of judgment.

"Then delay my end until the Day of their resurrection."

— Surah Al-A'raf, *7:14*

From this single act of misguided intoxication, alcohol manifests in the realm of physical examples as sinful and prohibited acts.

Satan learns about himself in a challenging way, which is why he harbors eternal animosity toward Adam. Conversely, Adam descends to experience opposites and understand the meaning of Goodness.

This comparison between goodness and good deeds (*Hassanat*) and evil and bad deeds (*Sye`at*) is emphasized throughout the Quran.

"Surely good deeds wipe out evil deeds. That is a reminder for the mindful."

— Surah Hud, *11:114*

Goodness is a rewarding status for those who consistently do good deeds.

"Is there any reward for goodness except goodness?"

— Surah Ar-Rahman, *55:60*

Artistically and realistically, the name of Allah in Arabic letters represents a cosmic calligraphy created by the Dot, conveying what was and what will happen and answering how and when the beginning occurred.

On Divine Veils and Revelation:

Allah describes Himself as Light. The dot reveals secrets within Allah's name. This hidden secret represents the essence of the creator, which remains unknown to the vast majority.

The Divine Dot manifests through veils and partitions. Veiling, or adding partitions to the secret, occurs through a descent process which is mentioned in:

"It is certainly We Who have brought down the Reminder, and it is certainly We Who will preserve it."

— Surah Al-Hijr, *15:9*

The process of unveiling is called Opening. In Surah Al-Fath, which translates as 'The Opening', Allah says: *"Indeed, We have granted you a clear opening."*

— Surah Al-Fath, *48:1*

Veiling was mentioned in Surah Al-Mutaffifin,

"Undoubtedly, they will be sealed off (Veiled) from their Lord on that Day."

Q — Surah Al-Mutaffifin, *83:15*

Others acknowledge the issue, humble themselves, and submit their will to God as they begin their search.

Where and how should one embark on the journey?

And how could the answer be closer than the jugular vein?

As Surah Qaf says:

"Indeed, We created humankind and know what their souls whisper to them, and We are closer to him than his jugular vein."

(Qur'an 50:16)

The divine essence of the name is concealed within its secret, and this essence can be accessed through the gate of that secret. All that is needed is to delve into the name and learn to read it properly under the guidance of an authentic sheikh.

The Prophet Muhammad (PBUH) provided a human analogy, referring to himself as the essence of the city of knowledge and to Sayyiduna Ali (PBUH) as its gate:

"I am the city of knowledge, and Ali is the city's gate."

(Hadith in Al-Tabarani, *Al-Hakim*)

13

Where is the gate of the divine name?

The gate is evident. Even an intuitive, tracing-based interpretation suggests that the circular letter 'Ha' (ه) is the gate.

The first word revealed to the Prophet Muhammad in the Qur'an was "Read" (*Iqra'*). However, there are differences between esoteric and exoteric reading methods.

The exoteric reading is visual, literal, and photographic.

The esoteric reading is exploratory, scanning, and gnostic.

An esoteric, exploratory reading of the name Allah in Arabic (ه ل ل ا) from left to right illustrates the gate methodology.

The fourth letter (*Ha* ه) is the gateway to the city of knowledge.

The third letter (*Lam* – ل) leads to another *Lam*.

It's as if the esoteric eye scans from left to right.

The second *Lam* leads to hidden knowledge, serving as a gateway to the fourth letter (Aleph – ا), symbolizing the return journey within the letters of Allah's name.

This return journey toward Allah is affirmed in Surah Al-Baqarah:

"Surely to Allah we belong, and to Him we will ˹all˺ return."

(Qur'an 2:156)

Most people interpret this verse metaphorically. However, exploring the Qur'an from various dimensions—especially literal and symbolic—suggests that the return journey is inherent in the name itself.

Key Points:

- Allah is not a body; rather, bodies embody His secret.
- The letters are the Dot's attire.
- Satan, who represents the reverse embodiment of goodness, was a mercy in disguise for illusory beings.
- Allah's mercy surpassed Satan's in the Garden, until Satan openly displayed his wickedness.
- Satan's self-awareness, as he conversed with the Lord, led to a state of intoxication—reflected in the forbidden acts outlined by Shariah, such as alcohol and fornication.
- Spiritual navigation (Sulook) refers to the journey from darkness toward the radiant name of Allah, progressing from Ha to Aleph, and finally to the Dot, ultimately reaching the Essence.
- Descent introduces multiple layers—from density to subtlety—while veiling obscures meaning. In contrast, opening serves as the key that lifts these veils.

The Dot Wrote the Name so We Can Read It

Chapter 3
The Name

How can someone confirm God's existence and know Him, rather than merely know about Him?

This puzzling question often leaves many searching for answers, as countless claims and often contradictory paths present themselves for exploration.

Throughout human history, religion has sought to provide answers. Organized religions and belief systems fundamentally differ in their physical and metaphysical aspects. However, they almost universally agree that the path to the metaphysical begins at the physical level— by following commands, avoiding prohibitions, and performing rituals. Subsequently, all aspiring Gnostics need to do is reflect on the name God revealed about Himself.

To understand this book seamlessly, the reader must pause at this paragraph and reflect on two intricate questions:

- What is the definition of a 'name'?
- How does the divine name differ from a human name in terms of definition?

Both human and divine names share the characteristic of depicting the essence of the name. Therefore, a name reflects the quality of the essence.

The naming process is one difference between a divine name and a human name. Parents choose a human name to reflect the anticipated qualities of the child; it is like putting the cart before the horse.

It is not uncommon for children to wish to change their names to align with their self-perceptions. A human name is part of a family tree whose origin dates back to Adam and Eve; however, most family trees are limited to five or six generations.

The human naming process is a pre-emptive attempt to denote a person's essence. A human's name is, so to speak, a wishful thought.

However, the revealed Divine Name is neither chosen by humans nor preselected to signify an essence. This book may argue that the Name uniquely reflects, mirrors, and leads to the Divine Essence. Since Allah revealed Himself, and since Allah is individual and indivisible, so is His Name. Nevertheless, the name in its letter format reflects an ethereal, moulded shaping of the essence's likeness as its meaning descends. This moulding is what the initial Pen wrote to transition from absoluteness to limitation.

How Has Allah's Name (ﷲ) Been Expressed Further?

The Name was revealed through a process of unveiling, highlighting multiplicity and diversification in three stages, which we can refer to as three magnificent, expansive worlds: **Jabaroot, Malakoot**, and **Mulk.**

One of the Surahs is titled *The Sovereignty* (Al-Mulk):

"Blessed is the One in Whose Hands rests [all] sovereignty (al-Mulk), and He is Most Capable of everything."

(Qur'an *67:1*)

Surah Ya-Sin mentions the Malakoot:

"So glory be to the One in Whose Hands is the dominion (Malakoot) of all things, and to Him you will be returned."

(Qur'an *36:83*)

This verse hints at the relationship between all things and the Malakoot dimension, as well as the path of return, all in one verse.

Although the term Jabaroot does not appear in the Qur'an, it is mentioned in Hadith and often linked with Malakoot in the same context:

"Praise be to the Owner of Jabaroot and Malakoot."

(Hadith Shareef)

"Glory to the Owner of Jabaroot and Malakoot, the Almighty and the Great." (Hadith Shareef)

Jabaroot signifies a supreme type of authority and power that allows for no duality.

These three worlds are vertically portrayed:

- The realm of invincibility (Jabaroot),

- The realm of illuminated spirituality (Malakoot), and

- The physical realm (Mulk or Nasoot).

In every realm, Allah's Name manifests differently; the lower the realm's position, the denser and more dispersed the name manifestations become.

These three realms signify the transition of meaning from subtle to dense, from overwhelming brightness to dark, rich representations of forms and shapes.

- The transition from meaning and subtlety to physicality and density created the illusion of space for the human mind.

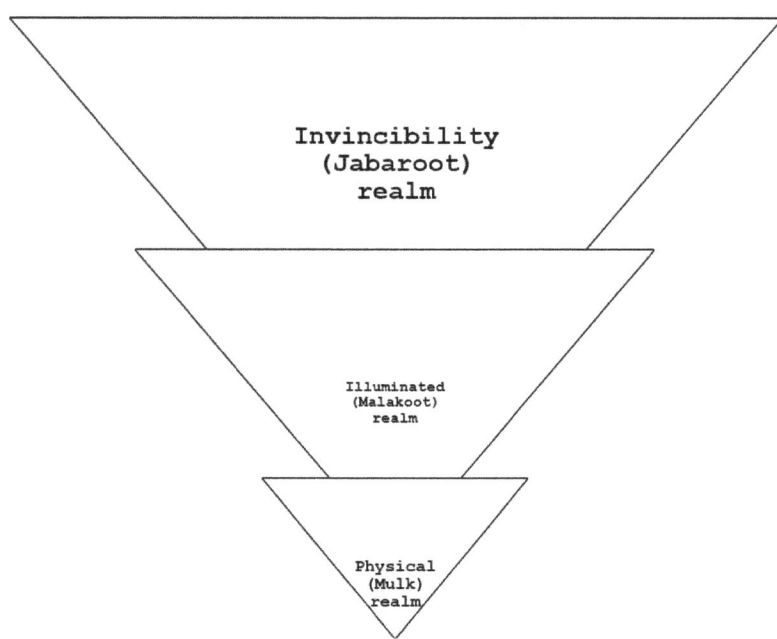

Allah's Name Revealed in the Realm of Invincibility

The domain of Allah existed alone, with nothing beside Him.

The Ethereal Pen, via the Dot, wrote the illuminated Name *Allah* (ﷲ).

This is the domain of Surah Al-Ikhlas:

"Say: *He is Allah, [who is] One."*

(Qur'an 112:1)

The Prophet ﷺ said about Surah Al-Ikhlas:

"By Him in Whose Hand my soul is, it is equivalent to one-third of the Qur'an."

(Bukhari: 6643)

The Jabaroot realm represents this one-third.

- In the physical realm, we are commanded to recite Surah Al-Ikhlas:

- "Say: He is Allah" (Qur'an 112:1) to emulate the Jabaroot primordial event in one of the three most subtle realms.
- In its esoteric revelation, Surah Al-Ikhlas represents the realm of invincibility, depicting the Divine Name as one of three aspects—the other two being the realm of illuminated spirituality and the realm of the physical world.
- Surah Al-Ikhlas is equivalent to one-third of the Qur'an.

The Name's Revelation in the Spiritual Realm

In this realm, the Name branches like a tree with a trunk of Oneness and 99 primary attributive branches, such as The Most Compassionate, Most Merciful, The King, and The Holy.

This is the domain of the concluding verses of Surah Al-Hashr:

"**He is Allah**—there is no god *but* Him—*the* Knower of the unseen *and the* seen. He is the Most Compassionate, *the* Most Merciful.

He is Allah—there is no god *but* Him—*the* King, the Most Holy, the Source of *Peace*, the *Giver of Faith, the Overseer*, the Almighty, the *Compeller, the* Supreme. *Glory be to* Allah far above what they associate with Him.

He is Allah—the Creator, the Inventor, the Shaper. *To Him belong* the Most Beautiful Names. Whatever is in the heavens and the earth glorifies Him. And He is the Almighty, the All-Wise."

(Qur'an *59:22–24*)

The Name's Revelation in the Physical Realm

Imagine a seeker of divine knowledge, sitting in solitude, meditating and mentioning the Name Allah (الله), immersed in Divine light.

"Say: 'Allah.' Then leave them to amuse themselves *in their false discourse."*

*(*Qur'an *6:91*)

What is 'Subhan' or 'Subhan Allah'?

The Arabic word 'Subhan' is often translated as glorify, yet its literal root conveys a motion of swimming.

One of the most frequently uttered words by Muslims is 'Subhan Allah', which may allude to swimming in the Divine Ocean of Light.

"So glorify *Allah in the evening and the morning."*

(Qur'an *30:17*)

This swimming of the Name by the whole cosmos is a form of glorification.

"Whatever is in the heavens and the earth glorifies Allah—for He is the Almighty, the *All-Wise."*

(Qur'an *57:1*)

23

This verse implies a kind of cosmic, swimming glorification across all realms.

- Allah asked the Ethereal Pen to write what was and what will be.
- The Pen wrote the Name.
- The Name Allah illuminates hidden reflections of His attributes.

- These manifestations of Allah's attributes are reflected in three distinct realms: Invincibility, Illumination, and the Physical.
- The attributes branch like a tree—each reflected in colours, forms, and shapes.
- The transition from subtlety to density created space, and the sequential unveiling of manifestations created time.

Chapter 4
Reading the name

The Quran's revelation first occurred during the Prophet Muhammad's usual retreat in the Cave of Mount Hira. It was there that the Angel appeared and instructed the Prophet to read. The Prophet's response can be understood in various ways: "I cannot read," or "What should I read?"

The first command, 'READ,' found in Surah Al-`Alaq from the Quran, is undisputed.

"Read, in the Name of your Lord Who created."

(Q *96:1*)

But what kind of reading was demanded?

Was it meant to be an exoteric reading—engaging the eyes, mental comprehension, and spoken words—or an esoteric interpretation, involving the heart's eye and internal senses, or merely the act of vocalizing words?

The instruction likely included all the above and more.

The main idea I want to convey is that there are countless reading methods available.

Exoteric versus esoteric 'reading':

The educational journey of exoteric reading through external senses is exemplified in early childhood education, with children advancing through stages that start with the acoustic phase, characterized by **hearing**, mimicking, and repetition. Utilizing visual aids during this phase enhances the educational process.

As children grow, they learn to read not only images but also the expressions on the faces of their parents and relatives.

As children grow, they can express what they have read in **writing**, completing the educational process by translating knowledge into images and shapes. This requires essential tools: a pen, ink, and a tablet.

Then, children can transfer knowledge by 'saying'; **saying** is the tongue's equivalent of writing, and it brings the educational cycle back to the visual phase, enhancing education among similar species.

Educational cycle: hearing, seeing, reading, writing, and saying.

Furthermore, proper schooling requires an appropriate location for basic education, unlike applied education, which is lifelong and not limited to a specific place or stage of life. This system, designed for humans, reflects the Divine educational system aimed at knowing God.

These educational steps are described in the Quran to connect exoteric learning to the internal journey of gnosis.

Humans have educational tools at both physical and metaphysical levels that match their developmental stages in physical and gnostic aspects, which do not necessarily progress in tandem.

The physical does not usually align with the gnostic age. It is possible to encounter a physically mature adult who remains a gnostic child, a knowledgeable scientist or skilled writer who lacks gnostic understanding and literacy, or a bright, thoughtful problem solver sinking into gnostic darkness and ignorance.

Immediately after birth, in a specific order of hearing followed by seeing, as demonstrated in Surah Al-Insan:

"Has there [not] come upon man a period of time when he was not a thing [even] mentioned?

Indeed, We created man from a sperm-drop mixture that We may test him; and We made him hearing and seeing."

(Q 76:1–2)

The birth of truth seekers occurs after they start the journey under the guidance of an authentic guru, even if that is in their last decade of physical age. They progress through spiritual childhood, teenagerhood, adolescence, etc.

Hearing the authentic guru's permission to embark on the journey is called the 'pledge of allegiance' (Bay'ah), and the verse of 'Bay'ah' is usually read during this stage of gnostic birth. This remains a contract between the esoteric seeker and the guru.

"Indeed, those who pledge allegiance to you [O Prophet] are actually pledging allegiance to Allah. Allah's Hand is over their hands. So whoever breaks their pledge, it will only be to their own loss. And whoever fulfills their pledge to Allah, He will grant them a great reward."

(Q *48:10*)

This stage of hearing and seeing is a prerequisite for the following educational steps, including esoteric reading and writing.

Surah Al-`Alaq summarizes the reading and writing stages. Once again, this should be interpreted as both esoteric and exoteric development.

"Read, in the Name of your Lord Who created.

Created humans from a clinging clot.

Read! And your Lord is the Most Generous,

Who taught by the pen,

Taught man what he knew not."

(Q *96:1–5*)

- Reading is not limited to words and letters; it also encompasses recognizing and naming shapes, artwork, gestures, and even intentions.
- Reading not only engages our external senses but also invites access through our internal senses.
- The facts referenced in the Quran—such as a person, a story, or a cosmic sign—signify certain realities that can be encountered on the spiritual journey.
- Similar to exoteric reading, esoteric reading has childhood and adult stages.

Esoteric Reading for Spiritual Seekers:

The life of Prophet Muhammad demonstrates a spiritual journey that serves as a guide to understanding God.

In the journey of spiritual navigation, hearing signifies the sheikh's permission in words.

Seeing represents witnessing the divine light. Reading embodies the seeker's interpretation of what they observe.

The writing pen may symbolize the tongue, subdued external senses, deeds, and actions.

School is a place of solitude, isolation, and spiritual retreat. Seeing is witnessing the illuminated name or divine light. Reading the illuminated letters.

Exoteric reading

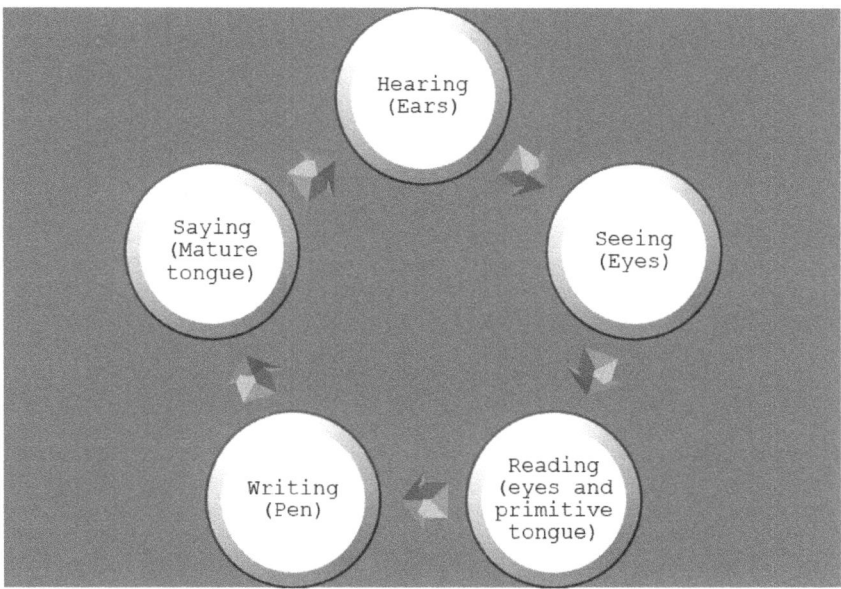

Esoteric reading, beginning:

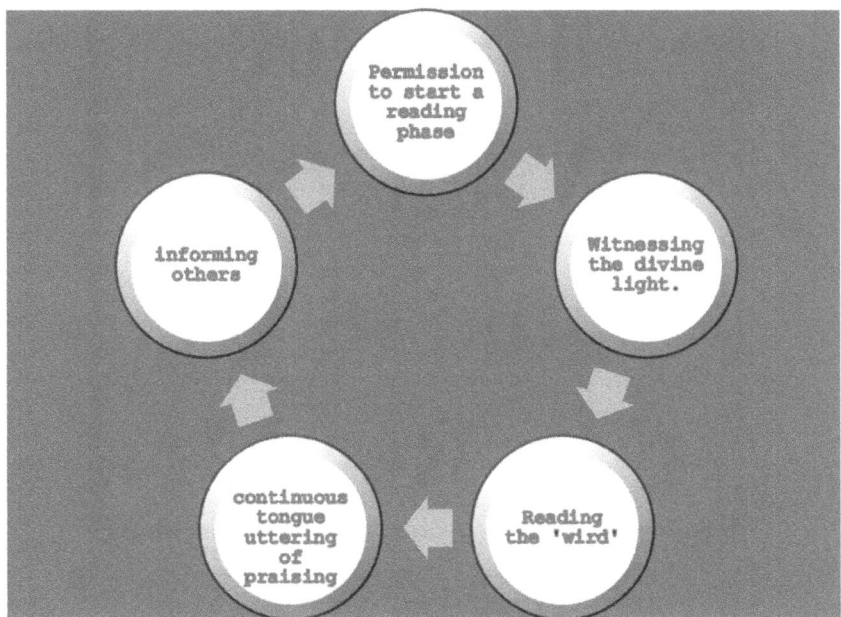

Esoteric reading, continuing:

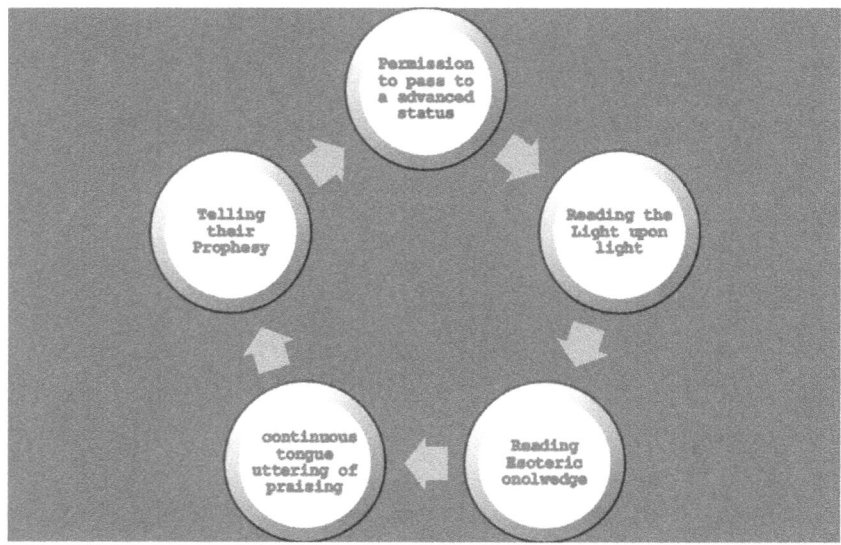

The Dot Wrote the Name so We Can Read It

Chapter 5: The Swimming Motion – The Intricacy of 'Subhan Allah'

It is not unusual for humans to ask existential questions during their search process, such as:

How did the life journey begin? How will it end? Is it fair to live with unknowns and the unseen components of belief? Is current life the only one that exists or will exist? Is God deniable because we cannot examine divinity under a microscope? If God is provable, is He always unseen until we die, and at what point can we verify Him? What are the tools of verification? Is it reasonable to apply the tools we know to uncover the truth we do not know? Will there be reward and punishment, and why? What benefit would reward and punishment bring to God? And if He already knows the outcome, why wouldn't He create a tale of everyone living happily now and ever after?

These are common questions that theologians encounter from their skeptical counterparts. How can one verify post- and pre-life if no one has been there and returned to tell us? Moreover, why wouldn't skeptics be aware of at least the pre-life component?

Nonetheless, the typical counter-questions are:

Does it represent a starting point and conclusion, or an endless cycle of exposure and concealment? Why can't the hidden play an educational role in divine revelation?

What if our lives represent a captured cycle of an eternal process? What if skeptics arrive at incorrect conclusions due to using unsuitable investigative methods?

Is God solely capable of hiding and remaining unseen, or can He also be evident and visible? What if we possess the tool within us? Do we exist autonomously?

What if we are the last remnants of a continuous series of observable events? Is existence a representation of divine names and attributes shown in an infinite, eternal cycle of manifestation and non-manifestation?

Finally, why do we believe that no one has traveled between pre-life and post-life to share their experiences? Aren't all metaphysical practices aimed at helping truth seekers transcend the illusions of time and space, with varying levels of success?

Why do we insist on calling the results of these experiences a phenomenon rather than using other means of knowledge acquisition? Don't historical records recount selected individuals claiming to have been present and trying to convey words or even written scripture to inform us—individuals whom we denied during their lives and after their departure? Moreover, how could anyone assert with certainty that they had been there? What if we have been, but do not remember? Don't we all experience partial memory loss from our childhood and most teenage years? Don't we have complete memory loss of our first five years of life unless we have reminders, photos, or fragments of stories? Don't we have complete amnesia for seven to nine months in the womb?

So, why wouldn't we explore what the Quran says about the atomic offspring's original testimony phase (**Alam al-Dharr**) when we all existed and declared a pledge of allegiance to the Creator before taking turns to appear in human form in the physical realm? In Surah Al-A'raf, Allah says:

"And [mention] when your Lord took from the children of Adam— from their loins—their descendants and made them testify regarding themselves. [He said], 'Am I not your Lord?' They said, 'Yes, we have testified.' [This]—lest you should say on the Day of Resurrection, 'Indeed, we were unaware of this.'"

(Q 7:172)

How is the human creation simulating the **Dot's** swimming journey?

The Dot's transcendence through the veils of the unseen into the realm of possibilities, akin to a drop from the ocean of divine words, is simulated daily in our lives thousands of times.

This occurs through the birth process, arising from the love between two individuals representing beauty and majesty, made of mud and divine secret duality. The process includes will, action, and motion, followed by a drop of seminal fluid evolving into a born child, then into an adult, aging, and ultimately returning to its origin. Humans often experience total or partial memory loss of the preceding phase and a hypothesis of the years to come.

The Quran mentions the detailed process in various verses. The rule of thumb is that if a fact is mentioned in the Quran, it signifies a more important truth in the esoteric journey back to Allah.

Even the reference to this mysterious Dot evolution was hinted at in the thematic verse of this book, the first few verses of Surah Al-'Alaq:

"Read, in the Name of your Lord Who created.

Created humans from a clinging clot."

(Q 96:1–2)

This verse illustrates a distinct and intricate stage in the revelation of the Dot, emerging from the ocean of the unseen into the realms of manifestation. It depicts a suspended drop that has passed through the Pen of omnipotence and is now poised to write the name of the Creator.

We can infer that everyone symbolizes the diffusion of the Dot into a mud vessel, and the purer the vessel, the closer its resemblance to the Dot's characteristics.

Allah created everything; nevertheless, humankind exists within a hierarchical system that requires a central entity of the highest quality. Similarly, the human dots should contain a central dot within them.

The Quran emphasized the reality of the centrality-and-periphery system, simulated by the marvellous beehive. The Quran even dedicated a whole chapter to this topic, titled The *Bees*.

> - This dot swimming-like motion writing the name (الله) reflects an esoteric meaning of 'Subhan Allah' (الله سبحان).
> - The Dot's journey through unseen layers into the realm of possibilities, akin to a drop from the ocean of divine words, is recreated daily in our lives and observed in the human journey from before birth to after death.
> - Every human is a Dot, but only one living human is the Dot.
> - Prophets and God's Friends (Awliya) of the time mirror the exact reflection of the DOT.

The Quran also provides a detailed description of the physically interpreted external creation that signifies the esoteric journey of the mysterious Dot. Surah Al-Mu'minun says:

"And certainly did We create man from an extract of clay.

Then We placed him as a sperm-drop in a firm lodging.

Then We made the sperm-drop into a clinging clot, and We made the clot into a lump, and We made [from] the lump bones, and We covered the bones with flesh; then We developed him into another creation.

So blessed is Allah, the Best of Creators.

Then indeed, after that you are to die.

Then indeed you, on the Day of Resurrection, will be resurrected."

(Q 23:12–16)

Esoterically, this verse illustrates the following:

> - The drop exemplifies the evolution of the mysterious Dot.
> - The secure place represents the domain of the Merciful Name.
> - The dots exhibit various behaviours—clinging, expanding, differentiating, and swimming—highlighting transcendent passages of cosmic creation.

"And We created above you seven layers [of heaven]. And We are never unmindful of [Our] creation."

(Q 23:17)

This verse highlights another aspect of the Dot's descent, influencing the rains that settle on the earth for reproduction:

"And We sent down water from the sky in due measure, and We settled it in the earth. And We are certainly able to take it away."

(Q 23:18)

Interpretation:

- The Mother's womb, Earth, and the Merciful Name are equivalents—manifestations of the Tablet (*Lawh*).

- The drop of rain, the drop of pregnancy fluid, and the planting of a seed are equivalents—manifestations of the Dot.

- The descent passage, the changing shapes of the embryo, the seven heavens, and the birth canal are equivalents—manifestations of the Aleph.

The entire process of cyclical exemplification is a 'Ha' manifestation.

> - It is reasonable to conclude that, without the 'Ha' boundary limit, the Aleph manifestation would have remained hidden.

Chapter 6
Spiritual Navigation (Sulook)

Theologians often face inquiries such as: What will the end be like? Why are eternal happiness and misery part of the scripted scenario? Is religion created to fill the void of the unknown? Is the concept of God a false assumption because we cannot prove it through experimentation or observe the subtle with a microscope? Is 'End' an illusion? Will the life-scripted scenario perfectly fit the roles everyone is serving? Or are we using the wrong microscope to draw a biased conclusion?

Existential questions have persisted since the early days of human reflection. While some philosophers have dedicated their lives to addressing a few, the most challenging is the **Epicurean paradox**. This paradox questions why an omnipotent, all-powerful God does not prevent evil from occurring, why a loving God allows evil to exist, and why an all-knowing, loving God would punish those He can easily forgive in a narrative of His own creation. Is the existence of evil and suffering contradictory to perfection?

The Epicurean paradox resonates better with individuals facing challenges related to calamities on personal, public, or eternal levels. It fails to comprehend the educational rule regarding the manifestation of evil and goodness in declaring divine attributes and merely captures and generalizes a still-framed snapshot of the bigger picture.

Omnipotency involves the capacity to allow opposites—such as goodness and evil—to unfold for the greater benefit of the system. This is achieved by maintaining a driving force behind change and improvement, encouraging humankind to strive for problem-solving and to learn more about divine characteristics indirectly.

The continuous transition between calamity and pleasure enhances humankind's progress and evolution through a relentless urge for change.

At times, the argument reaches a dead end, and philosophers persist in denying God. Meanwhile, religious scholars argue that God exists because He stated so and does whatever He wishes.

The argument culminates by questioning why God wouldn't reveal Himself to us.

This book will argue that God has revealed Himself and continues to do so, and one of the most profound revelations of Allah's essence is revealing His name.

The Quran concludes the creation process in Surah Ya-Sin:

"His command, when He intends a thing, is only that He says to it: 'Be!' – and it is. So exalted is He in Whose Hand is the realm of all things. And to Him you will be returned."(Q 36:82–83)

The journey summarized:

- Divine will
- Lordship 'Command'
- Divine quote: 'Be'
- The outcome: 'Being'
- The forms: Things
- A zoomed-out view: The spiritual realm (Malakoot) features vast cosmic swimming orbits, hinted at by the word **'Subhan'**. This showcases the movement of created entities within a non-physical or spiritual realm (Malakoot world).
- Return phase: The journey is not a one-way ticket but a round trip

How does the Lordship command manifest in the physical (Mulk) realm, which is hypothetically lower than the spiritual (Malakoot) realm?

Surah Al-Hadid:

- Explores the answer to this question and demonstrates swimming capability in the physical (Mulk) realm
- Confirms the dual opposing divine capabilities, such as being the First and the Last, and allows contradictions—like life and death—to manifest and exist

"Whatever is in the heavens and the earth glorifies Allah, and He is the Almighty, All-Wise.

To Him belongs the dominion (Mulk) of the heavens and the earth. He gives life and causes death, and He is Most Capable of everything.

He is the First and the Last, the Manifest and the Hidden, and He is All-Knowing of everything.

It is He who created the heavens and the earth in six Days, then established Himself on the Throne. He knows what enters the earth and what emerges from it, and what descends from the sky and ascends into it. And He is with you wherever you are. And Allah is All-Seeing of what you do.

To Him belongs the dominion of the heavens and the earth. And to Allah all matters are returned.

He merges night into day and day into night, and He knows what is hidden in the chests."

(Qur'an 57:1–6)

What does spiritual navigation (Sulook – سلوك) mean? What does it signify?

Spiritual navigation (Sulook) represents a spiritual journey that transitions from delimitation to non-delimitation. In this context, the journey is the destination, with arrival signifying being and staying on the journey.

Is the path during spiritual navigation visible?

Yes. It is visible and has stations, motels, post signs, and landmarks.

Navigating this path in the first life—when mercy prevails—saves time and hardship compared to navigating the same path on the Day of Judgment, when oppression and sovereignty predominate.

Is the Sulook path mentioned in the Quran?

Not only mentioned, but also read and recited numerous times each day by the average Muslim. Without reciting it, the obligatory prayer is incomplete.

Reciting Surah Al-Fatiha in each unit of the obligatory Muslim prayer is mandatory. This results in Al-Fatiha being recited at least 17 times a day. The last verse out of seven in Surah Al-Fatiha asks to be guided to the Straight Path:

"Guide us to the Straight Path. The path of those You have blessed— not those who have earned Your anger or gone astray."

(Q1:6–7)

In the afterlife, this Straight Path becomes a bridge that everyone must cross to reach safety. It becomes clearly visible in the afterlife, while remaining internal and hidden in the first life as the spiritual navigation (Sulook) route, for both those who have been blessed and those who have gone astray.

Spiritual navigation (Sulook) involves tracing the journey backward from density to subtlety, and transcending through the divine name, from what eyes can read to what the heart can see.

What is the purpose of spiritual navigation (Sulook)?

The Quran combines analogies of traveling the Straight Path with the journey of reading a book. This makes the concept of spiritual navigation particularly fascinating, as navigators are simultaneously traveling their path and reading the book they have already authored.

"We have bound every human's fate to their neck. And on the Day of Judgment, We will bring forth a book that will be laid open.

Read your book. *You alone are sufficient this Day to account for yourself."*

(Q 17:13–14)

*"On that Day, We will roll up the heavens like a **scroll of writings**. Just as We produced the first creation, so shall We reproduce it. That is a promise binding upon Us. We will truly fulfill it."*

(Qur'an 21:104)

*"The revelation of this **Book** is from Allah, the Almighty, the All-Wise. Indeed, We have sent down **the Book** to you in truth. So worship Allah, being sincerely devoted to Him."*

(Q 39:1–2)

- The purpose of spiritual navigation is to **trace the divine command's journey backwards.**
- The Sulook journey transitions from density to subtlety, exploring divine ability to encompass opposites: concealment and revelation, manifestation and non-manifestation, stillness and movement, and the creation of life.
- The divine command was formed, shaped, universalized, historicized, embodied, spatialized, and represented chronologically.
- While searching their internalized divine command, spiritual navigators recognize that **they themselves are the books** they have been searching for in the vast external world.
- This **bookkeeping of divine commands** led to the creation of many books covering time, space, history, the universe, and personal prophetic legacies. Furthermore, the divine commands were also documented in scrolls.

The verses in the textualized divine command scrolls resemble tree branches stemming from a trunk that originates from a seed holding a mysterious secret of production.

Some consume the tree's fruit (casual readers); others explore knowledge by contemplating a branch's creation (scientists and thinkers); while some examine the intriguing seed (verifiers). Spiritual navigators seek to understand the seed's delicate power.

While most passersby enjoy the fruit's taste, a small number assert that the seed offers a subtler flavour that surpasses the fruit itself. Spiritual navigators are part of this latter group.

Personalization of the divine command:

The backward tracing of the divine command is represented historically by the journey from the Adamic, earthly characteristics of Adam (PBUH) to:

- Noah's era, when humanity reached an irreparable state of anti-lordship rebelliousness, necessitating drastic measures through the flood for the story to progress

- The revival of monotheism by Abraham

- The challenging spiritual navigation and self-struggle in the history of Moses and the sons of Jacob

- The risk of fleshly temptation during the journey of Joseph

- The climactic extreme subtlety of Jesus

- And finally, the collective appearance of the Prophet Muhammad, peace be upon them all.

Chapter 7
The Textual Spiritual Navigation

The history of the textual book:

The Quran informs us that the original divine command was revealed in stages through various texts, including the **scrolls** of Abraham, the **Torah** of Moses, **the Psalms** of David, the **Gospel** of Jesus, and the **Quran**, which compiles and elaborates on all of them.

"Indeed, this is certainly ˈmentionedˈ in the earlier Scriptures—the Scriptures of Abraham and Moses."

(Q 87:18–19)

"Indeed, We revealed the Torah, containing guidance and light."

(Q 5:44)

"And We have surely favoured some prophets above others. And to David, We gave the Psalms."

(Q 17:55)

"Indeed, We have sent revelation to you ˈO Prophetˈ as We sent revelation to Noah and the prophets after him. We also sent revelation to Abraham, Ishmael, Isaac, Jacob, and his descendants—as well as Jesus, Job, Jonah, Aaron, and Solomon. And to David We gave the Psalms."

(Q 4:163)

The **Bible of Jesus** (or the **'Injeel'**) is mentioned several times in the Quran. For example, Surah Al-Ma'idah describes a Day of Judgment scene:

"And ˈrememberˈ when Allah said, 'O Jesus, son of Mary! Remember My favour upon you and your mother: how I supported you with the Holy Spirit so you spoke to people in your infancy and adulthood. How I taught you the Book, wisdom, the Torah, and the Gospel. How

42

you moulded a bird from clay—by My Will—and breathed into it, and it became a real bird—by My Will. How you healed the blind and the leper—by My Will. How you brought the dead to life—by My Will. How I prevented the Children of Israel from harming you when you came to them with clear proofs, and the disbelievers among them said, "This is nothing but pure magic."

(Q 5:110)

This gradual revelation of the textualized command aligns perfectly with the prophetic historical journey of the command's humanized or personalized aspects and spatial representation, from the subtle characteristics of the skies and heavens to the density of the Earth.

The Quran and the textual spiritual navigation:

The Quran is the book of all books and the written version of the universal book. The first verse after the opening chapter (Al-Fatiha) states undisputedly and clearly that the Quran is not *a* book, but *the* book.

*"**This is the Book**! There is no doubt about it—a guide for the pious."*

(Q 2:2)

The spiritual navigator sees the Quran as a book that displays divine command, with 'Allah' (الله) as the book title. Therefore, learning how to read the name 'Allah' (الله) is the shortest straight path to verification.

Delving into the name Allah may surprise truth seekers or spiritual navigators by showing how Allah tells the story from beginning to end using four Arabic letters, one of which is a duplicate.

- Before starting with the 'name reading,' it is essential to understand what 'name' signifies, what 'reading' involves, and what letters indicate.

Letters are lines formed by countless ink dots and manifestations of a dot creating shapes. They allow the ink dot to express itself, demonstrating its ability to impart life through a secret flow into shapes and lines.

The same concept applies to a colourless source of light, which becomes colourful by altering frequencies and generating colours.

Therefore, it is reasonable to conclude that letters and colours are illusions created by a supposedly silent, quiescent, hidden, unseen, colourless, illuminating dot with immense capabilities to manifest itself as the opposite of what it is presumed to be. As a result, life arises from pseudo-lifelessness, letters arise from a dot, and colours emerge from colourlessness.

This logic illustrates that truth seekers aim to understand the original, illuminated, colourless (yet colour-giving), motionless yet fully capable Dot, or the Primordial Light or Muhammadian Reality.

The name 'Allah' in Arabic, represented by the flowing ink dot, symbolizes countless occurrences of the same dot in the creation of time, space, the heavens and earth, civilization, and history.

This gradual dispersion of the dot manifestations creates countless systems of tree-like configurations. This tree begins as a straight stem, resembling Aleph in Arabic letters, and branches emerge from the Aleph, taking various curvatures that signify the other letters, which are merely different manifestations of the Aleph. Letters are expressions of the Aleph, and the Aleph is an expression of the Dot, while the Dot can encompass all opposites and subtly flow through all the letters. The Alphabet is a tree with a stem (the Aleph) and a seed (the ink Dot).

This stem and branch analogy will be brought to a marvellous reality show on the Day of Judgement, when we all must prostrate to the collective stem. This is mentioned in the often mistakenly translated verse of Surah Al-Qalam:

"That Day the Shin will be uncovered, and they will be called to prostrate, but they will not be able—eyes humbled, humiliation

covering them. For they had been called to prostrate while they were sound."

(Q 68:42–43)

(Note: "Shin" is the literal Arabic "sāq" [ساق]—often symbolically interpreted as "stem" in mystical readings.)

> - Spiritual navigation is a journey from the circular manifestation of the 'Ha' to the linearity of the 'Aleph'.
> - Allah illustrated this journey through the legacy of every prophet.
> - The transition from 'Ha' to 'Aleph' has an initial **horizontal** followed by **vertical** metaphors.

The horizontal transition from Ha to Aleph:

The Minor Struggle

The first category can be viewed as metaphorically horizontal, encompassing stages such as searching and roaming (pre-Ha phase), seclusion (Ha), struggle (Lam), knowledge acquisition (Lam), and ultimately spiritual opening (Aleph).

Along this horizontal journey, spiritual navigators encounter and confront the representations of their inner selves within the physical world. This challenging period for the truth seeker is a battle against their individualized selves, as mirrored by the people and landscape surrounding them.

In this phase, the term 'Ha' signifies a tangible location—like a cave, a prayer corner, or a well—as referenced in Joseph's story, or even the belly of a whale (Jonah), Noah's Ark, and the cave of Hira for the Prophet Muhammad.

The dual 'Lams' signify the simultaneous acquisition of self-knowledge through adversity and challenges, including ridicule, battling an enemy, persecution, illness, coping, and confronting poverty—as particularly illustrated in Job's narrative, and the forced immigration of the believers out of Mecca during the Prophet Muhammad's (PBUH/HF) time.

The Aleph phase of the horizontal stage of spiritual navigation signifies shortcuts and straightforward physical-realm success and victory. It is represented by:

- A stick that splits the sea in Moses's story,
- The return sea journey in Jonah's story,
- Running in healing water in Job's story,
- The Ark's passage in Noah's story,
- The desert road of migration during the Prophet Muhammad's (PBUH/HF) time.

- The horizontal and vertical transitions from the 'Ha' to the 'Aleph' are repetitive and exhibit the same features, but they manifest in different ways.

- Any gateway to a new phase is considered a new 'Ha' that will lead to another intriguing 'Aleph' representation.

The vertical transition from Ha to Aleph:

The Major Struggle

The horizontal format is essential for vertical navigation to take place. The vertical navigation is the literally illuminated phase of spiritual navigators. The struggle here is against their own selves. During this phase, the navigators face three enemies: Self, Satan, and self-serving bias.

During this phase:

- The Ha of seclusion becomes visible as a niche of illumination.

- The Lam manifests as a spirit, and the navigators may see their souls before them.
- The other two 'Lam' letters become the longing fires of the love of the Creator and the gifted knowledge.
- The Aleph becomes an ascendant passage towards the Dot.

The Dot ascends to light upon light.

This vertical navigation phase is explained beautifully in the Quran in Surah An-Nur:

"Allah is the Light of the heavens and the earth. The example of His light is like a niche within which is a lamp—the lamp is in a glass, the glass is as if it were a brilliant star, lit from a blessed olive tree, neither of the east nor of the west, whose oil would almost glow, even if untouched by fire. Light upon light. Allah guides to His light whom He wills. And Allah presents examples for the people, and Allah is All-Knowing of all things."

(Q *24:35*)

- The Ha's act as portals to various departure points for the spiritual traveler.

- 'Ha' may manifest as a cave or hidden spot, an esoteric niche or a radiant circle (Mishkat), a journeying sphere of light (Soul or Rooh) that draws one upward, a hand of light (Qabdah), or an infinite brightness layered upon brightness.

Spiritual navigation made easy in the Prophet Mohammad's Legacy:

The narrative of the Prophet Mohammad's night journey describes how, against the laws of physics, he travelled horizontally from Mecca to the Al-Aqsa Mosque in Jerusalem in a single night.

Following this, he ascended through the seven skies, recounting his encounters and experiences beyond the throne.

The event is referred to as 'Israa and Mi'raj', which consists of navigating horizontally from the Ha to the Aleph and then vertically from the next 'Ha' at Al-Aqsa Mosque to the heavenly Aleph.

This remarkable story offers immense comfort to spiritual seekers, particularly during nighttime meditation when they may encounter similar experiences.

Chapter 8
The Aleph journey downwards

Reflection on Adam and Eve's story

Contemplating the Aleph is a vertical journey that leads to the enigmatic ink's Dot. The Dot serves as the portal to the Hidden Secret of the essence.

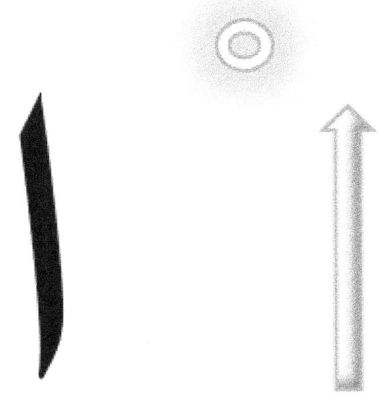

The Aleph narrates a tale of divine succession from the highest to the lowest realm. The pinnacle symbolizes the absoluteness of non-delimitation, serving as the dwelling of the enigmatic Dot, and this apex symbolizes the first revelation of the Dot's secret, highlighting the unlimited divine. It can be conclusively stated that it embodies the domain of prophecy.

Conversely, the lowest revealed facet of the Aleph is where the Dot is shrouded by clay, adopting a human form. This setting becomes an ideal location for Adam to explore and navigate the duality between the Dot's sacredness and the upward-pulling gravity, contrasted with the weight of earthly mud. This point illustrates this prophecy through text, specifically in the Message realm.

- The spiritual navigator ascends vertically within the Aleph.
- The message transforms from text to illuminated, symbolic, and colourful signals.
- The message appears different, more symbolic, more lucid, and less dense.
- The mind struggles to acknowledge that a more efficient means of internal exploration exists and that this route is just as apparent as the external one.

Belonging to both ends of the Aleph, Adam needed to come down to Earth to obtain his formal education and start learning about his lower origin in order to learn about his higher one.

On Earth, the revelation is abundant in text. Adam and Eve needed to align their lower tools with their higher equipment to gain and translate knowledge and complete tests; they would receive promotions and obtain the seal of approval. They also had to keep their sound belief and do only good deeds to avoid further descent to the lowest of the low.

"Indeed, We created humans in the best form. Then We reduced them to the lowest of the low, except those who believe and do good—they will have a never-detached reward."

(Q 95: 4-6)

Every travel journey requires a traveller, a driving force, direction, signs, a destination, hurdles, a façade, a compass, motels, stations, luggage, and carry-on bags. It also necessitates a will, senses, a vehicle, a companion, a guide, affordability, and natural capability. A perceived sense of progression creates the concept of chronology and time, while a change in scenery demands the spatial tool of space.

The mind doesn't readily accept that not only is there a more effective means of internal travel available, but that this path is just as visible as the external one.

Internal travel or spiritual navigation utilizes internal senses, using the soul as a vehicle, piety as food and clothes, fuel of remembrance of the creator, road signs of star, sun, and moon, stations of submission (Islam), belief (Iman), and perfection (Ihsan), and the motels of fear, honesty, love, and longing.

The Quran described this as tourism, wandering on the earth, or travel, and gave many hints that this travel breaks the barrier of time and place and allows one to see what happened in the past and even the original realities.

"Say, "Travel throughout the Earth and see how He originated the creation, then Allah will bring it into being one more time. Surely Allah is Most Capable of everything."

(Q 29:20)

In Surah Al-Hajj, earthly travel serves as a means to open and engage the internal senses, particularly unlocking the unlimited capabilities of the heart's eye:

"Have they not travelled throughout the land so their hearts may reason, and their ears may listen? Indeed, it is not the eyes that are blind, but it is the hearts in the chests that grow blind."

(Q 22:46)

This verse clearly indicates that the heart possesses an eye, and that true blindness impacts this internal eye rather than the external, physical one.

However, it is crucial to emphasize that opening the heart's eye demands alignment between physical and spiritual journeys, and the façade must be unified for a fruitful enlightenment. If the façade is comprised of lust and desires, the flesh will dominate the soul, leaving the heart blinded despite the efforts.

The unification of the soul and the driving force of the flesh, known as the self, represents the pinnacle of Islam. This aligns with the declaration of the first pillar of Islam, expressed as "La Elaha illa Allah", meaning There is no deity but God.

When the Self and the Soul sync and work together, and both external and internal senses align, messages from their default guiding 'Internal Messenger' commence.

This internal messenger is mentioned in Surah At-Tawbah.

*"There certainly has come to you a **messenger from among yourselves**. He is concerned by your suffering, anxious for your well-being, and gracious and merciful to the believers."*

(Q 9: 128)

Spiritual navigators' grand prize is seeing this internal messenger with the heart's eye, whether awake or asleep. Only once they see him can they say inside out that "Mohamad Rassoul Allah," or the messenger of Allah, is Mohammad, thus completing the first pillar of Islam, known as the testimony (Shahada).

How about other prophets that came before Muhammad (PBUH/HF)?

Exploring the context of reality and verification, the internal messenger symbolizes the essence of divine messengership. Thus, **all the prophets are one undivided reality** under the singular truth known as 'Mohammad.'

*"The Messenger believes in what has been revealed to him from his Lord, and so do the believers. They all believe in Allah, His angels, His Books, and His messengers. **"We make no distinction between any of His messengers."** And they say, "We hear and obey. 'We seek' Your forgiveness, our Lord! And to You 'alone' is the final return"*

(Q 2:285)

Consequently, the historical prophetic figures reflect various facets of this reality, from Adam's balanced Adamic nature to Jesus's pure, holy-spirited essence.

Vertical journey of truth within the Aleph

- Upright Aleph

- From subtlety to density

- From non-comparable to parable.

Spirit/Subtlety/Heavens/ Prophecy/light/meanings/intangibility

Clay/Mud/Earth/Density/ message/text/shapes/forms/planets

Horizontal historical journey of the truth within the Aleph:

- Horizontal Aleph
- From clay to spirit
- The horizontal ascendance

Adam (clay)→Noah→Abrahim→Moses→Jesus (spirit)

- The significant historical prophetic figures showcase different aspects of this Mohammadian reality, ranging from Adam's harmonious clay nature to Jesus's sacred spirit essence.

Where is the message realm located on the Aleph?

The message realm, representing the lowest revealed point of the Aleph, requires messengers, while the prophecy realm, depicted at the apex of the Aleph, necessitates prophetic knowledge or prophets.

In Islam, every messenger qualifies as a prophet and might carry a text scroll, yet not all prophets are messengers. Figures like Abraham, Moses, Jesus, and Muhammad held both titles and had the authority to fulfill both roles.

In Surah Maryam, Moses and Ishmael are specified as both prophets and messengers, whereas Arona and Enoch served only prophetic roles.

*"And mention in the Book **Moses**. He was truly a chosen man and was a **messenger and a prophet**."*

(Q 19:51)

*"And We appointed for him—out of Our grace, his brother, **Aaron**, as a **prophet**."*

(Q 19:53)

*"And mention in the Book, **Ishmael**. He was truly a man of his word and was a **messenger and a prophet**."*

(Q 19:54)

*"And mention in the Book, **Enoch**. He was surely a man of truth and a **prophet**."*

(Q 19:56)

In contrast, figures such as David, Solomon, Lut, Jacob, and Hud were solely prophets and behaved accordingly.

It is essential to highlight that, in Islam, all prophets and messengers are flawless and incapable of committing intentional sins, and that prophets and messengers are special individuals selected by God to guide and enlighten humanity in its educational pursuit of comprehending Him and valuing His companionship and presence.

Lineage purity:

Since Adam's time, the purity of the physical lineage has been maintained within chosen families to ensure that their divine secret aligns and is preserved within the purest inherited physical vessel.

Allah upheld a steady approach by ensuring a pure lineage of selected guides from Adam and Eve. This family heritage enlightens humanity and signifies the manifestation of the primordial Dot in human existence.

*"Indeed, Allah chose **Adam**, **Noah**, the **family of Abraham**, and the **family of 'Imrân** above all people. They are descendants of one another. And Allah is All-Hearing, All-Knowing."*

(Q 3:33-34)

The Dot Wrote the Name so We Can Read It

Chapter 9
The Nadir of the Aleph

The story of Adam and Eve

Adam and Eve strayed away from the abundance of direct, effortless, and seamless learning in the Garden, which reflected the dot's delicate spiritual nature, to the challenging and distant process of gaining knowledge more suited to the clay form of the Dot on Earth. Yet, they weren't alone in facing this decline. Satan was also demoted from his status of residing in the higher kingdom to the realm of physicality and shapes.

Losing his status was a blow to Satan's pride. His ego prevented him from facing reality. In his elusive mindset, he deceived himself and failed to recognize that Adam's creation provided him a chance to gain insight into himself and his circumstances.

Adam and Eve swung from promotion to demotion, disobeying to repentance, from guaranteed luxury to hard work to survive, from drawing near to expelling far, and finally from being spoon-fed divine nurturing of lordship to learning by doing servanthood.

"So We said, "O Adam! This is surely an enemy to you and to your wife. So do not let him drive you both out of Paradise, for you would suffer. Here, it is guaranteed that you will never go hungry or unclothed. Nor will you suffer from thirst or 'the sun's' heat."

(Q 20- 117-119)

They emerged from childhood without the responsibilities of childhood and exhibited teenage characteristics of forgetfulness and naivety. They experimented with what they were not allowed to do by getting close to the tree and falling into a trap, and subsequently into disobedience. Then, they were removed from the house and had to learn and support themselves.

"And We once made a covenant with Adam, but he forgot, and We did not find determination in him."

(Q 20:115)

They gained insights from their experiences about how desire can cloud judgment, recognizing the initial indicators of falling as nudity and the erosion of modesty and dignity.

"So lured them through deception. And when they tasted of the tree, their nakedness was exposed to them, prompting them to cover themselves with leaves from Paradise. Then their Lord called out to them, "Did I not forbid you from that tree and ˙did I not˙ tell you that Satan is your sworn enemy?"

(Q 7:22)

Satan was a critical example of what being bad looks like. He was the embodied nature of arrogance, jealousy, and pride; he was the master of illusion, lying, manipulation, and a lifelong enemy to Adam and Eve and their offspring. Satan to them was a living red light, an evident indicator of the notion to stop. They were told to simply obey, or otherwise, they would be cursed by distancing themselves from God for an unknown period.

- Allah taught Adam the collectivity of his names, and Adam emerged as the instructor to the angels regarding their creator's names.

- Satan refused to bow down and take the pledge from Adam.

- A dialogue took place between God and Satan, allowing him to explain.

- Eve was created from Adam. She represented the beauty.

- Allah warned Adam that Satan was his eternal enemy and never to approach a specific tree in the Garden.

- Satan could not suppress his evil nature and continued to attempt to lure Adam and Eve with one goal: to lead them to the tree.

- Satan exploited Adam and Eve's naivety using the mechanism for forgetfulness they possess.

Disobedience or forgetfulness:

Adam forgot Allah's warning, believed Satan's claims, drew closer to the tree, and ate from anywhere in that heaven. He acted according to his nature and his inherent forgetfulness and weak resilience.

"And indeed, We once made a covenant with Adam, but he forgot, and We did not find resilience in him."

(Q 20: 115)

- Adam asked for forgiveness, and he was forgiven. Hence, Islam opposed the idea of divine sacrifice or the concept of inherited sins.

- Satan did not ask for forgiveness. He debated and rationalized.

Losing Humility:

Adam and Eve were surprised by how drastically their nature had changed, how their appearance had become exposed. They were shocked and then embarrassed to see their lower halves and to experience desire and hunger. They hurried to cover themselves with leaves from the garden.

At this moment, they realized that everything they had once acquired with ease—food, enjoyment, modesty, and even clothing—would now demand hard work and effort.

Adam discovered the importance of making mistakes, dealing with forgetfulness, practicing repentance, and, most importantly, securing basic needs such as food and clothing. On the other hand, Satan learned about his elusive characteristics and from that point forward, both were ready to embark on their learning journey from afar.

The divine command came to Adam, Eve, Satan, and the supporting angels to descend to the lower kingdom.

Emergence of religious laws and regulations:

Courtesy of the experience and the subsequent hardships and repentance, Adam and Eve matured. They understood causation, consequences, modesty, the educational function of lordship, and the presence of adversaries and enemies. Now, they are ready to implement the Lordship skills they have acquired.

They can utilize their knowledge to assist children experiencing similar yet distinct phases of development: from childhood to adolescence, adulthood, and eventually independence, only to enter the cycle again.

Eve learned she would be the earth that would give birth; her womb would be the garden that continuously supplements life.

They learned how to be forgiving yet assertive parents, guiding and directing while expecting their offspring to forget and make mistakes.

At the end of the journey, they would become complete, perfect humans worthy of the status given to them, which is also higher than angels.

Adam and Eve were parents to two sons, Qabeel and Habeel, born from two different pairs of twins. Qabeel inherited sinful traits, while Habeel embodied the pinnacle of goodness and unrealistic forgiveness. Soon, Qabeel's evil characteristics manifested in anger, jealousy, and greed. He eventually killed Habeel and buried him, a practice he learned from observing a crow burying another. Qabeel, heeding his evil traits and succumbing to the misleadings, eventually separated and rejected all the laws.

How was the clay purified?

How does the straight Aleph become delimited in a circular Ha?

It is easy to understand that a highly subtle Fist of Light or a mysteriously divinely crafted Dot is pure. The home or the simulation laboratory for this Dot or such a fist of light is clay from the deepest point.

The Quran explains the process of preparing a vessel to host the Dot from Dust to Dust.

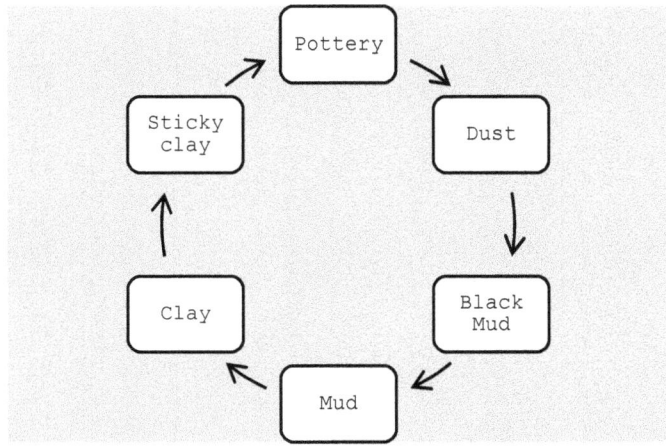

*"One of His signs is that He created you from **dust**, then you turn skin-enclosed beings spreading"*

(Q 30:20)

*"We said to the angels, 'Prostrate before Adam,' so they all did—but not Iblîs, who protested, 'Should I prostrate to the one You have created from **mud**'."*

(Q 17:61)

*"Your Lord said to the angels, 'I am going to create a human being from sounding clay moulded from **black mud**'."*

(Q 15:28)

*"Who has perfected everything He created. And He originated the creation of humankind from **clay**."*

(Q 32:7)

*" So ask them, which is harder to create: them or other marvels of Our creation? Indeed, We created them from a **sticky clay**."*

(Q 37:11).

*"He created humankind from 'sounding' clay like **pottery**."*

(Q 55:14)

Process of death before and after life:

62

Direction of gravitation of the dual senses:

The integration of external and internal senses, physical expressions, rituals, navigation routes, and light with mud occurs through the unification of the façade (Qiblah).

Religious practices require this façade for prayer, which represents the physical aspect of creating a divine connection, much like how each sensory group functions as a 'Facade'.

"Indeed, We see you with your face towards heaven. We will make you turn towards a facade that will please you. So, turn your face towards the Sacred Mosque wherever you are, turn your faces towards it."

(Q 2:144)

The primary elements of the human creation:

Dust, water, fire, and air illustrate the subtle forces of Divine knowledge: the command to bring life into existence with the word 'Be', the passionate fire of love for creation, and at last, the powerful, holy breath.

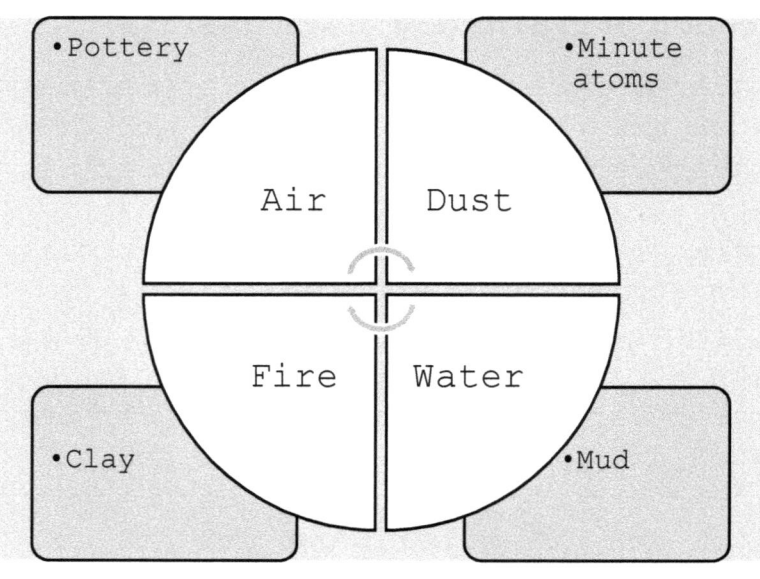

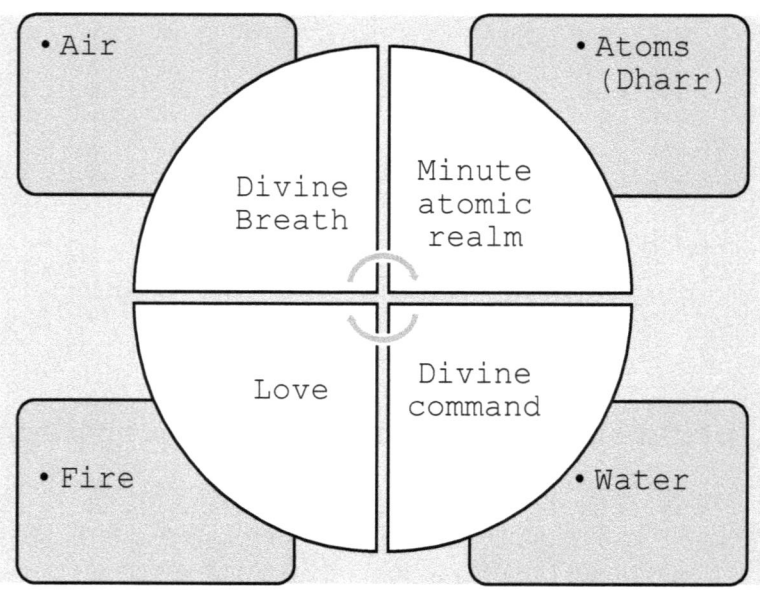

Surah Al-Hajj eloquently summarizes the entire journey from dust to a detailed description of development in the womb, through birth, and into this world of ours, which is full of illusions, until death. The verse concludes with a parable that exemplifies how the Earth mimics the creation and 'impregnation' story.

"O humanity! If you are in doubt about the Resurrection, then We did create you from dust, then from a sperm-drop, then a clinging clot, then a lump of flesh—fully formed or unformed—to demonstrate to you.

'Then' We settle whatever We will in the womb for an appointed term, then bring you forth as infants, so that you may reach your prime.

Some of you die, while others are left to reach the feeblest stage of life so that they may know nothing after having known much.

And you see the earth lifeless, but as soon as We send down rain upon it, it begins to stir and swell, producing every type of pleasant plant."

(Q 22:5)

The Pure Duality Family:

The pure essence of the original Dot, representing the pinnacle of elevation, combined with the water and fire and refined clay from the depths, created the finest expression of humanity, where the low mirrors the high. Allah implemented this system within a family lineage from Sheth to Noah, to Abraheem.

From Ibraheem, the message branched into two paths. One was the lineage of Isaac and his son Jacob. Jacob, known as Israel, had sons mentioned in the Quran as the Sons of Israel, and a dormant branch of the Prophet Ismael.

During the Abrahamic era, sacred books and scrolls emerged, preserving the original message in written form. Nevertheless, written messages still require a human translator, interpreter, or messenger.

In the Islamic view, the human counterpart and the written message were passed down through Jacob's descendants until the era of Jesus. Within Islamic theology, Jesus is recognized as both a messenger and a prophet. This belief maintains that Jesus was not killed; rather, he remained alive and ascended to the second sky, where he is expected to return.

Ibraheem had scrolls, Moses had books and the Torah, and Jesus came with the Bible. Yet all the original books were written in languages that perished. They either became rarely used or entirely non-existent. Consequently, ordinary people had to rely on translations when access to primary sources was limited. Gradually, these translations prevailed, allowing for variability and distortion. Limited access to the original text and language posed a risk of political influence on scholars and allowed for deviations—subtractions, additions, and mistranslations—from the original meanings.

Following Jesus, this family tree system was interrupted, and the divine message shifted from the Sons of Jacob (or Sons of Israel, descendants of Isaac) to the dormant lineage of Ismael, which upheld monotheism in the Arab peninsula, and ultimately to the Prophet Muhammad PBUH/F. The last written message took form as the Quran, and the final embodiment was the Prophet Muhammad PBUH/F.

From an Islamic Sufi and mainstream Islamic perspective, the established divine system continues until the end of time through the finest lineage of the Prophet Muhammad (His family). This tradition prompts Muslims to honour him with the title PUBH/F or Peace be upon him and his family.

The Quran, being the final lasting message, is crafted in a living poetic language that rhymes and is inherently easily memorable. This ease of memorization of the Quran has allowed for its preservation and kept it intact. The fact that Arabic is a language that is alive and well used further contributes to the Quran's memorability.

This approach serves as a divine means to sustain both a message and a language—the message's memorability enhanced through rhyme and the promises of rewards for every letter pronounced fueling the devotion and will to spare no effort in keeping the message intact. It is truly remarkable, and I find it captivating.

Chapter 10
The Aleph

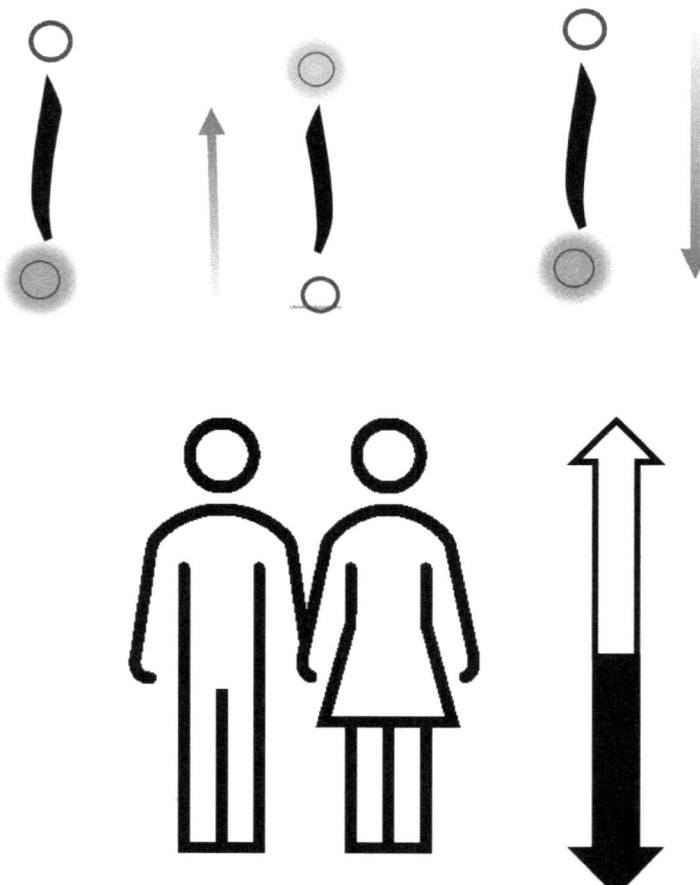

The truth seeker must discriminate between the original, straight, partially revealed entity "written" by the Pen via the Dot (the Original Aleph); the various replicated images or traces of the original Aleph in the universe and among creatures, as manifested in the cosmic structure; and to keep in mind that humankind is created from two opposing forces, each possessing its own armies and soldiers.

"To Allah belong the soldiers (forces) of the heavens and the earth. And Allah is Almighty, All-Wise."

(Q 48:7)

"Then the idols will be hurled headlong into Hell, along with the deviant; and the soldiers (forces) of Iblîs (Satan), all together."

(Q 26:94)

Being of different origins, each army is drawn to its roots. Managing this everlasting battle is called the Major Struggle (*Jihad Akbar*), or self-struggle.

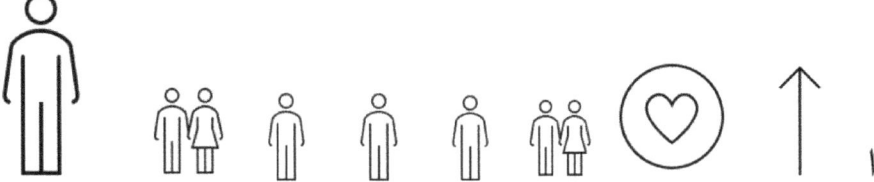

The illuminated army within gravitates upward.

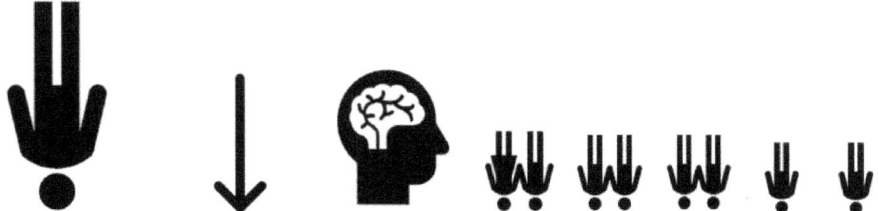

The dark army within gravitates toward the Earth.

Surah Al-Mulk provides a perfect description, illustrating the guided person who walks upright (i.e., a vertical Aleph) along a straight path (i.e., a horizontal Aleph). Meanwhile, misguided individuals move with their faces touching the ground and gravitating downward.

"Who is more guided: the one who crawls facedown or the one who walks upright on the Straight Path?"

(Q 67:22)

The mind commands an army made up of the external senses of sight, hearing, touch, movement, and taste, thriving on pleasure and desire. It demands continuous gratification from food and sexual needs and is drawn to the earth from which this army originally emerged.

This army plays a crucial role in maintaining human procreation and sustainability. It also provides a starting point for the return journey and dwelling of the Aleph nadir.

Satan's primary job is to control and overwhelm the mind with conflicting thoughts and questions, seeking to declare independence from divine law (Sharia). Subsequently, the mind begins bribing its soldiers with indulgence in food and desires, refuses to submit to the heart, and a journey into forbidden descent continues until the soldiers hit rock bottom.

This is the path that was followed by Satan, keeping him under the curse of distance until the next day of creation or the Day of Judgment.

This army comes from Earth, is attracted to earthly things, and after death, Mother Earth engulfs it and returns it to its origin. As a mother, Earth will either give a warm, welcoming embrace or a painful, reprimanding squeeze. At the time of death, this army of external senses and "mud products" will have to face its own actions and be accountable to a "happy" or "unhappy" mother, so to speak.

If this army follows the continuously descending **footsteps of Satan**, it becomes an evil force.

"O believers! Do not follow the footsteps of Satan. Whoever follows Satan's footsteps surely invites immorality and wickedness. Had it not been for Allah's grace and mercy upon you, none of you would have ever been purified. But Allah purifies whoever He wills. And Allah is All-Hearing, All-Knowing."

(Q 24:21)

They become allies of Satan's lowermost kingdom. On Judgment Day, Satan will claim those who willingly followed him and failed to control their earthly bodies made of mud and clay. His dwelling will not be a pleasant or comfortable place for those he views as enemies.

"He said: 'Do you see this one you honoured above me? If You delay my end until the Day of Judgment, I will certainly take hold of his descendants, except for a few.' Allah responded, 'Be gone! Whoever of them follows you, Hell will surely be the reward for all of you—a fitting reward.'"

(Q 17:62-63)

Thus, death could be defined as the return of each human component to its origin.

Conversely, the illuminated, sublimated human beings and soldiers are drawn upward to the Spiritual Illuminated World (Malakoot). They are always searching beyond metaphysics, submitting to a sound heart, and striving to defeat the earthly forces within. They employ their internal senses, see through the heart's eye, thrive on God's praise, and realize that the only way to win this struggle is to shackle the opposing army's foot soldiers of external senses.

The army's strength increases when it abstains from excessive food to deny gluttony its flavor, adheres to guidelines in sexual relations to resist the temptations of its adversaries, and ignores life's superficial distractions and desire triggers to diminish the mind's false sense of power.

We can refer to this army as the Army of Illumination, the Heavenly Army, the Divine Allyhood Army, or the Army of Light.

After death, this army should ascend to where it belongs. However, this requires complete detachment from the earthly realm. Such detachment is the goal of every Sufi navigator.

Without a complete and undisputed victory of the army of light over the army of darkness, there will remain strings attached after physical death. One may correlate this with Qur'anic verses that refer to victory, as this army seeks to claim the landscape of the senses and the body in order to ascend into the illuminated world.

The Individual's Triumph and "the Land"

The **triumph** achieved and the perspective gained are entirely internal, reflecting what humanity has consistently struggled for throughout history: the land. For truth seekers, "the land" symbolizes their external perceptions, serving as a means for ascendant movement.

One can read the Quran in this way to extract a personal message on an individual level.

"And victory comes only from Allah; the Almighty, All-Wise."

(Q 3:126)

"Allah has promised those of you who believe and do good that He will certainly make them successors in the land (earth), as He did with those before them."

(Q 24:55)

Truth seekers begin their educational journey by verifying the Aleph's impact on themselves, the universe, or the physical world (Al-Mulk) through emulation, authentic rituals, and adherence to specific character traits.

This path requires external senses, reflection, and sincere prayer. It encompasses the dos and don'ts of Islam (Sharia law), allowing for metaphorical thinking. The heart is trained to guide the mind effectively. However, this carries risk, as the mind might deceive the heart into a false sense of sovereignty.

This serves as a caveat for anyone embarking on the journey without a guide or Sheikh. Without a sound heart, one cannot progress to the next step.

At this juncture, the truth seeker requires approval from an authentic Sheikh, either to advance to the next level or to continue further practice to attain a **sound and healthy heart**.

"The Day when neither wealth nor children will be of any benefit. Only those who come before Allah with a sound heart."

(Q 26: 88-89)

The next step for the truth seeker is to ascend into the spiritually illuminated world. This is metaphysical, not merely metaphorical.

This path relies entirely on the awakened internal senses and the heart's eye (Basirah). It entails complete control over the external senses, which are strongly attracted to the physical, visible world.

The Journey of Aleph Verification

- Emulating the Aleph in the physical world.
- Reclaiming the external senses from the mind's sovereignty.
- Engaging in self-struggle against the lower self or the earthly dark army within, to strengthen the internal illuminated forces.
- Winning battles, if not the entire war.
- Applying the rules of the physical world to restrain the external senses.
- Awaiting the awakening of the internal senses under the guidance of a sound heart.
- Ascending in the spiritually illuminated world, both awake and asleep.
- Achieving annihilation in the Dot.
- Verifying the Dot.

The Aleph is one of the expressions of the Dot; writing the Aleph resulted in creation and spatiotemporal impact.

- The Dot masterfully inscribed the Aleph with stunning elegance, embodying the initial revelation of divine essence.
- The Aleph mirrors its images in creation, branching outward.
- The traces of these trees can be found universally, with each being distinct, as Allah's representations are always unique.

The Command	Divine Breath	Transcendence	Meaning		Worldly Manifestations	Perceivability
	Primordial light	Ahmadian reality	Encompassing Surpassing characteristic	Mercy	World of invincibility (*world of Jabaroot*)	Shock and awe. Annihilation (*Fanaa*)
	7 Heaven	Abrahamic reality	Friendship/Companionship characteristic			
	6 Heaven	Moses's reality	Vocal characteristic			
	5 Heaven	Aron reality	Expressive characteristic		• World of illuminations.	
	4 Heaven	Idrees reality	Inscribing characteristic		• Seven Heaven locations.	Internal senses
	3 Heaven	Joseph's reality	symbolic decoding characteristic		• World of spirituality (*World of Malakoot*).	
	2 Heaven	Jesus's reality	Spirit characteristic			
	1 Heaven	Adamic's reality	Opposing gathering characteristic			
	0 Earth (First Earth)	The pottery embodied reality	Parable characteristic		• World of physical beings (*World of Mulk*).	External senses

75

○	Commands Brain matter	Heart	Throat (Holqoom)
١	Movements and functions formation Spinal Cord and electrical impulses, and biochemical cascades	Aorta	Esophagus
	Lower spinal cord point	Thoracic aorta	Diaphragmatic dome
○		Aortic division	Stomach and intestines
			Balance and nutrients separation
			Impurities

Human Tree and Aleph Model

The Aleph tree is rooted in human creation. When discussing human creation, we begin with the physical body and then transcend to the metaphysical.

The Aleph's primordial cosmic motion ripples and replicates traces that eventually reflect in the spinal cord, which extends from the brain's height to the mid-back. Before spreading its roots, it is protected within the hard clay of the spinal vertebrae.

The spinal cord creates its own tree as it descends and branches out. The spinal cord tree resembles a top-down flow of an ink dot, creating Aleph calligraphy with a dot located at the top. This dot at the top is an Arabic symbol called Hamza, which resembles a small "cap."

The spinal cord shape resembles a tree planted in heaven, with branches that descend. This top-down model also appears in other creations.

Conversely, the heart-and-aorta model features an upward representation of the Aleph Tree. The aorta symbolizes the Aleph, while the heart signifies the Dot. The remainder of the left circulatory system forms the tree's branches.

The Galaxy Tree

The sun's beams of light and rays illustrate the flow of the Aleph's secret in the universe, while the stars represent distant branches. The stars resemble the nerve endings of the cosmic sun or the capillaries of the solar heart.

The Selected and Purified Trees

- For books: The Qur'an.

- For humankind: The family tree from Adam to Seth, to Abraham, Moses, Imran, and the family of the Prophet Muhammad.

- For seeds: The black seed (described as a cure for every illness).

- For trees: The olive tree of Mount Sinai.

- For animals: The dog from the People of the Cave.

- For food: Honey.

Not all trees are equal. The uniqueness of the Adamic tree illustrates that replication can produce inferior trees and that not all trees hold the same status.

Contamination occurs at every level. Not all olive oil is superior, and not all honey is curative; human "trees" can be contaminated as well. For example, some of Adam's offspring followed Satan's footsteps and produced a mixed lineage carrying impurities.

Allah's mercy dictates that a pure, default tree is preserved at the spiritual and genetic levels. Therefore, being connected to this tree and drawing closer to it serves as a remedy for contamination.

Similarly, honey is the purest form of nectar, and olive is the purest form of oil. The prophetic cascade of each era represents the pure tree embodying humanity's highest Aleph sacred flow. The prophetic tree of our time comprises the chosen elites of the Prophet Muhammad's family, as inherited through the family of Imran during the time of Maryam and Jesus (peace be upon them).

Chapter 11
Reading the Name

Tracing Allah's name in Arabic illustrates the roadmap and step-by-step directions for returning to God. This roadmap repeatedly presents itself in different contexts of time, place, history, the sequence of the sent prophets and messengers, universal constructs, and more.

The first word of the first verse revealed to the Prophet Muhammad (PBUH/HF) was READ:

*"Read in the name of your **Lord Who** created."*

(Q 96:1)

What Does "Reading the Name" Mean?

Is it the visual recognition of the three Arabic letters that comprise the name of Allah: Aleph (ا), Lam (ل), and Ha (ه), which together form the name Allah (الله) ?

Or is it about knowing how to identify and pronounce it?

Or does it involve engaging in utterance and meditation, mentally recalling, verbally expressing, and yearning for closeness to the Divine?

In the Sufi path, all the preceding steps are mandatory, combined with self-struggle against heedlessness and distractions, repentance, maintaining purity, and following the instructions provided in the holy books—those revealed by the prophets and messengers.

However, these are not considered **true** reading. Rather, merely attempting to read and perceive the written letters or uttering them aloud is not truly seeing or speaking.

In this phase, seekers are blindfolded and mute, mistakenly believing they are seeing and speaking eloquently.

So, what is true reading?

What are the indicators of true vision, proper speech, and sound thinking? Are there signs?

Are these signs standardized so that one may benchmark oneself against other seekers?

Accurate reading begins only after practicing all preliminary steps. To the seeker's surprise, two events unfold: illuminated signs start to appear on the internal path within the seeker's heart, revealing universes, shapes, and forms that the seeker never imagined the heart could contain.

Then, seekers realize how many years they have wasted searching externally and understand that the answer is within, closer than their jugular vein. The interaction with these illuminated signs becomes an internal dialogue, confirming the nearness of the Divine, who is, or was, too close to be seen, veiled only by the person's ego, desires, lower self-needs, and mental idols.

For those who can esoterically interpret the Qur'an, these signs are referred to as SIGNS. Anything described as a sign in the Qur'an represents a reality on the internal roadmap and an external example on the horizon.

I will describe a schematic, phased-out approach to the journey toward true reading, giving examples of a few signs that seekers should recognize. Without internally seeing these signs, seekers remain in the phase of self-struggle and cannot claim to read from a spiritual navigation perspective.

Schematic phased-out approach:

1. **Drowning Phase: The Internal Dark Sea**

   o   Utters words, closes eyes, and sees nothing but darkness.

   o   Indicates that significant work and self-purification are needed to survive drowning in the internal dark sea of ignorance, the tidal waves of arrogance, desires, and self-bias.

   1. If this phase is not recognized as a great danger, there is little hope for the seeker to navigate the ascending path of return.

2. **Surfacing: The Internal Stars/Sky**

   o   Sees stars in one's lowest internal sky.

   2. This is the first reassuring sign pointing the way to the surface of the inner sea.

3. **Sailing**

   3. A single guiding star shines in the middle of a clear sky, indicating guidance and the movement toward sailing in the proper direction—the journey of return.
   4. **Initial Ascending: The Internal Niche**
   5. **Middle Ascending: The Glass of Different Colors**
   6. **Unification and Monotheism: The Moon (Lamp Phase)**
   7. **"As If You See Him" Phase: The Sun (The Lamp)**
   8. **White-Out Phase: Light Upon Light**
   9. **Self-Death and Vanishing: The Phase of the Vanishing of All but God**

Phases **2** through **9** are considered, in the **Sufi path**, to be stages of **witnessing or *Shahada*.**

One of the intriguing aspects of the Sufi path is observing people practicing dry rituals yet becoming frustrated with others who are not like-minded—those who may be absorbed in heedlessness, work, careers, and family plans, and who have not yet experienced the beauty of verifying divine wisdom.

People in religious sects and fanatical groups create wars and spread terror, yet they have not understood or lived the first word of the first verse revealed in the Qur'an: READ (*Iqraa*).

Others judge who will be in Hell and who will be in Paradise, yet they have neither lived nor verified the first word of the first pillar of Islam: I WITNESS (*Ashhadu*).

This raises a fundamental question about the meaning of the Shahada—the declaration that there is no God but God—in Islam.

The reader of this book can reconstruct the phases of Shahada in Islam, moving from merely uttering the words to actual internal witnessing.

Capturing the Journey Back and Forth

External Reading Phase

- Involves studying the name through the external senses.

Focuses on tracing, scribbling, and maneuvering the letters, as well as the sequential order of writing the name from right to left.

One should master this phase repeatedly until the name becomes imprinted in the mind.

The roadmap to the divine secret involves tracing it backwards, as the gateway to knowledge begins with the last letter rather than the first.

Inscribing the name illustrates the sequence of revelation. Reading from left to right represents the return journey to the Divine Dot.

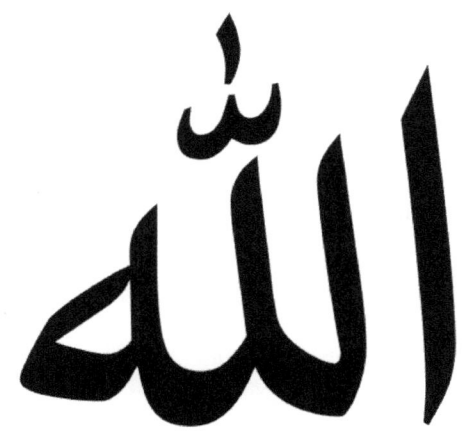

In an authentic hadith, the analogy of creation refers to a Pen that Allah created and commanded to write what had been and what will be.

By logical similarity, this metaphor suggests that a pen requires an ink-like substance to write. The drop of ink presumably summarizes the story in three formulas:

- **Delimitation**
- **Non-delimitation**

Non-delimited delimitation

These three categories shift from the realm of meaning into the tangible world in a gradual process, progressing from extreme subtlety to greater density.

The transition from subtlety to density occurs in three distinct phases, moving from the realm of meaning to the physical world. This progression highlights the relationship between these categories and illustrates how they evolve from one state to another.

This transitional shift is illustrated in the human realm of scripted letters as:

- Aleph → delimitation
- Ha → non-delimitation
- Lam → the intermediary link

Consequently, the Lam serves as the symbolic intermediary of all things.

In this model, Archangel Jibril (Gabriel) is seen as the intermediary link—the Lam—conveying a specific subtle message to the Cave of Hira, which symbolizes the Ha of non-delimitation.

The Dot Wrote The Name So We Can Read It

Chapter 12
The Dot

The Creator perceives no difference between beginning and end. Conversely, humanity experiences a gradual revelation of concealed truths. Vertical revelation fosters an illusion of space, whereas horizontal changes evoke a sense of time and history.

> Time and space are experienced illusions on the path to unveiling what is timeless and spaceless.

- o This initial reality is singular and whole, combining opposites and remaining non-delimited. It can be quiescent yet capable of motion; hidden yet visible; incomparable yet parable. It acquires "thinghood" through divine command, but there is nothing like this thing; nothing like it. It is non-embodiable yet simulated by bodies. It is colorless yet manifests in colorful illumination.

What does the dot represent?

- o The mysterious ink drop used by the ethereal Pen wrote what was and what will be.
- o The secret behind the metaphysical, extraterrestrial expressive motion of the divinely commanded "Be."
- o The straight-line motion that revealed the first letter of the name Allah, or Aleph, which is a straight, endless line that is partially apparent.
- o The flow of the calligraphic ceremony.
- o The unveiling, igniting force of Allah's name (الله).
- o A seed that blossoms into a blessed olive tree (or an oily, blessed tree).

85

- A subtle, mysterious entity that precedes the metaphysical, clinging, hanging drop.
- The momentum of the "Be" command reflects the secret of the lordship command.
- The holy ink drop of the ethereal Pen that wrote the Aleph, Lam, and Ha.
- Both the original mind and the foundational collective reality.
- A fertile seed as well as the olive-oiled, self-igniting, blessed tree.
- The gatherer of opposites and the ethereal calligrapher.
- A thing that has no likeness.
- A divinely selected (virgin) purity.
- The family tree of Noah, Abraham, Isaac, Ismael, Jacob, Imran, and the family of the Prophet Mohammad, who are all chosen and purified. *"Indeed, Allah chose Adam, Noah, the family of Abraham, and the family of 'Imran above all people."* (Qur'an 3:33)
- The essence that flowed through Maryam's womb and appeared in Jesus.
- The first dot in the Qur'an (the dot of the "Ba").
- The Dot is the purest of the selected black seed (not any black seeds), which has a cure for every illness (الحبة السوداء).
- The purest form of honey is believed to have medicinal properties for people.
- The preserved, protected, unchangeable divine message.
- The beginning and the end, and the manifest and the non-manifest representation of the divine attributes.
- The one and only "He," representing the pronoun "He."
- The face of the Merciful.
- The intermediary between parable and non-comparable.

- The origin of numbers, letters, shapes, forms, planets, and creatures.
- The embodiment of perfection in humankind.
- The collection of sayings by the Prophet Mohammad (PBUH/HF) to all humankind.
- S. Ali (PBUH), S. Al-Khidr during the time of Prophet Moses, and the man who knows the Book during the time of Prophet Solomon.

The Dot Wrote The Name so We Can Read It

Glossary

- **Aḥadiyya (Oneness)**: The state of divine singularity, emphasizing Allah's uniqueness and indivisibility.
- **Alam al-Jabaroot (Realm of Invincibility)** – The transcendent divine dimension beyond human comprehension.
- **Alam al-Malakoot (Spiritual Realm)** – The higher metaphysical dimension that the seeker journeys through for divine knowledge.
- **Alam al-Mulk (Physical Realm)** – The material world is governed by rules and regulations, preparing individuals for higher spiritual understanding.
- **Alaqa (Hanging or Clinging Drop)** – A stage of pure spiritual growth, symbolizing the developmental phase of the self.
- **Allah**: The supreme and only deity in Islam, whose attributes, essence, and manifestations are explored through creation and revelation.
- **Bedaa (Heresy or Innovation)** – A term used to accuse illuminated individuals of deviating from traditional knowledge.
- **Day of Gathering**: The eschatological event where all beings are resurrected and held accountable for their deeds.
- **Disclosure (Tajally)**: The unveiling of hidden divine realities.
- **Divine Essence (Dhat Allah)**: The core, incomprehensible being of Allah, beyond attributes and manifestations.
- **Divine Letters**:

- **Duality (Lordship/Servanthood)**: The relational aspect of Allah as the Lord and humankind as servants, reflecting a dynamic interaction.
- **Dust:** A state of creation referenced in the Quran before the formation of Adam and Eve, where these tiny ethereal particles observed and affirmed the existence of the ultimate divine reality.
- **Earth**: A massive seven-layered structure, akin to the seven layers of heaven, could be esoterically represented as projected onto the human body and flesh.
- **Embryonic Phase**: A metaphor for humanity's early state, likened to an embryo immersed in the divine amniotic fluid of praise and worship.
- **Façade (Qiblah):** The unified focus on the targeted goal. Represented by the Kaaba for prayer, the sheikh for followers, and the divine face for esoteric seekers.
- **Fana (Annihilation into Divine Essence)** – The ultimate phase of self-realization, where the seeker dissolves into divine awareness.
- **Fasl (Disconnection)** – The state of lacking spiritual connection, often represented by people of wickedness.
- **Furqān**: The recognition of divine traces in the dispersed manifestations of creation.
- **Ha**: The last letter of the name Allah in Arabic, when read from right to left.
- **He** (Howa): Means 'Him' in Arabic. Sufis use the term 'He' for God when referring to a specific divine character, acknowledging their ineffability in describing Him.
- **Heart (Qalb)**: The spiritual center of a human being, containing divine secrets and capable of ultimate divine perception.

- **Heavens**: Seven stacked layers of the massive upper structure of the cosmos. People at the top of the Earth see the lowest layer.
- **Iblees**: A creation that embodies everything good seekers should avoid. It was formed from smokeless fire, and the human eye cannot perceive him and his species. He is therefore considered an invisible enemy who masters deceit and can whisper ideas and thoughts into the minds of humans, making them vulnerable to his influence.
- **Injeel**: A book that was given to Jesus.
- **Jihad al-Nafs (Struggle Against the Self)** – The internal battle against desires and shortcomings.
- **Lordship (Rubūbiyya)**: A divine relational system representing the Creator's nurturing and sustaining role in relation to the creation.
- **Multiplicity (Shirk)**: The state of polytheism or associating partners with Allah, in contrast to divine unity.
- **Non-Manifest Names (Batin Names)**: Divine qualities not revealed to humankind, representing hidden aspects of Allah's essence.
- **Numerology**: The science of referencing letters within number systems.
- **Orbit (Falak)**: The divine boundaries within which each creation operates.
- **Pledge of Allegiance:** A promise-based agreement between the sheikh and the followers to uphold their obedience to God and to perform their daily meditations.
- **Pre-Atomic Phase**: A spiritual state preceding physical creation, described as a sea of light and divine knowledge.

- **Primordial Light (Muḥammadian Light)**: The foundational divine light, central to creation and representing Allah's attributes.
- Prophet: A person who does and is capable of telling about divine prophecies.
- Prophethood: A job and occupation of telling and informing one's own species about divine knowledge.
- **Prostration of Angels**: The acknowledgment of Adam's divine knowledge and representation of Allah's names by the angels.
- Psalms: Book of David
- **Sabeqoon (Forerunners)** – The highest-ranking spiritual seekers, leading the righteous path.
- **Sacred Phase**: A pre-material and holy stage in human existence characterized by divine praise, worship, and remembrance.
- **Satan (Iblis)**: The entity symbolizing ignorance, arrogance, and denial of divine authority.
- Scrolls of Abraham: books of Abraham to his people.
- **Servanthood**: The state of being a servant to Allah, characterized by worship, submission, and learning through divine guidance.
- **Tajelliyat (Divine Disclosure)** – The unveiling of hidden divine realities.
- **The Book (Kitab)**: The record of deeds presented on the Day of Judgment, encapsulating human actions.
- **The Hidden Secret (Sirr)**: Allah's essence, which remains incomprehensible and transcendent to human understanding.
- **The Trust (Amanah)**: The responsibility given to humankind to act as stewards of Allah's creation and uphold divine principles.

- **Thing-hood (Marḥalat al-shayʾiyya)**: The phase where humankind emerges as distinct entities composed of elements like clay, fire, water, and air.
- Torah: Book of Moses
- **Unification (Tawheed)** – The ultimate realization that all manifestations stem from a singular divine reality.
- **Witnessing (Shahada)**: The act of testifying to Allah's Lordship and recognizing His sovereignty.

www.ingramcontent.com/pod-product-compliance
Lightning Source LLC
Chambersburg PA
CBHW051223120626
46547CB00013B/1475

* 9 7 8 1 9 7 0 5 6 3 3 8 2 *